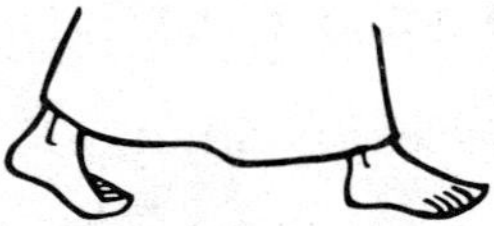

WAYS OF PRAYER SERIES

Basil Pennington, OCSO

Consulting Editor

Volume 8

Christian Yogic Meditation

by

Swami Amaldas

Michael Glazier, Inc.
Wilmington, Delaware

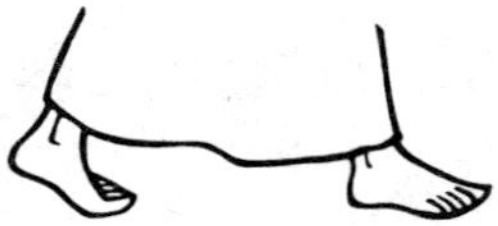

Published in 1983 by Michael Glazier, Inc., 1723 Delaware Avenue, Wilmington, Delaware 19806 *and* Dominican Publications, St. Saviour's, Dublin, Ireland

Library of Congress Catalog Card Number: 83-81844
International Standard Book Number:
Ways of Prayer series: 0-89453-282-0
CHRISTIAN YOGA
0-89453-368-1 (Michael Glazier, Inc.)
0-907271-28-6 (Dominican Publications)

Typography by Richard Reinsmith
Cover design by Lillian Brulc
Printed in the United States of America

CONTENTS

PART III

PART IV

PART V

PART VI

PART VII

Introduction

Yoga is the way to physical, mental, psychological and spiritual integration of the whole person. It is the harmony within oneself, between man and God. The whole purpose of Yoga is to grow gradually in Yogic Consciousness. In my last book *Yoga and Contemplation* I dealt with Astanga Yoga, the eightfold path of Yoga, from the Christian point of view and emphasised more the method of Hatha Yoga. In this book I am going to share with you the method of Christian Yogic meditation. The Christian Yogi in this sense is one who grows in Yogic consciousness in and through Christ Consciousness. This book is especially for Christians who are already initiated into the Christian way of life. I am writing this from my personal experience of Christian Yogic life. I believe very strongly that I must teach only what I experience in my life and what I believe I will be able to practice in the process of life.

There are three important stages in this method of meditation. The first stage tells how to grow in Christ Consciousness and through Christ Consciousness to Cosmic Christ Body Consciousness by singing the mantra of the sacred Name 'Om Nama Christaya'. The second stage tells how to use the breathing in and out, the natural life movement, as a means to enter into the eternal life movement between God and man through Yeshu Abba (Jesus — Father) Consciousness, the great mantra Yē and Ā. Through this method one grows into the conscious movement or relationship between man and man, between man and nature, between man and God. The third stage of this method tells how to experience the supernatural life movement, the inner life of God within oneself, that is the experience of the Trinitarian life of God, the movement between the Father and the Son in the Spirit, through the mythological symbolism of the serpent power 'Kundalini Shakti'.

The whole art of Christian Yogic meditation is the mystical marriage between the male and the female, 'Purusha and Prakriti'. As in any religious spirituality Christian Yoga also emphasises that the mystical marriage or union of man with God can only take place through the experience of death and life, the Paschal Mystery. The beatific vision, the experience after death 'Charamapadam' will take place only after death. But while we are in this life we can undergo the experience of death consciously. How far one undergoes the experience of death, so far one experiences God.

Often in Christian spirituality the physical and psychic aspect of the person is neglected. In Christian Yoga we believe that the physical and psychic aspect of the person has to be developed for him to experience spiritual enlightenment. One has to undergo physical and psychological healing in order to experience the transformation of the whole person.

The various exercises which are given in this book will help a person to make use of his own faculties, senses, intellect, reasoning and thinking in order to transcend time, matter and space and to enter into the ultimate silence beyond thoughts, words, ideas, concepts, theology, names, etc., to where one's spirit meets with the Supreme Spirit, where one experiences God in Spirit and Truth.

The book *The Child and the Serpent* by Jyoti Sahi influenced me a lot. I have made use of some of the ideas in this book in the chapter on Kundalini Shakti Yoga. I also studied under him while I was doing theology in Jnana Deepa Vidyapeeth, Papal Atheneum, Pune. I am ever grateful to all my teachers in Yoga as well as in theology. My thanks are due to all those who inspired me to write this book especially the people who have learned from me this Christian Yogic meditation.

With the blessings of my Guruji Father Bede Griffiths and my parents I wish that more and more people grow day by day in Yeshu Abba Consciousness. Let everyone breathe in and breathe out the love, joy and peace vibrations of the Holy Trinity.

In Yeshu Abba Consciousness
SWAMI AMALDAS

PART I

PART I

1. *A Call to Cosmic Christ Body Consciousness*

In 1968 in the second year of my Ashram life one day I sat on the top of a mountain in meditation posture and started to sing the Name 'Om Nama Christaya'. In the beginning naturally I kept my eyes open watching the sunrise. Through the rising sun I could see the mountains and valleys and people who live there. After some time the eyes were closed, the mouth too and the singing of the Name of Jesus continued in the heart with the breathing. Gradually I began to feel that my body was becoming bigger and bigger and finally the whole universe outside became my body. I saw that all that I had seen was inside me; the whole creation, the mountains and valleys; the whole of humanity; all the creatures; and the sun and moon and stars. I was taken into a level of consciousness where I experienced "My body is Jesus Christ's body and my blood is Jesus Christ's blood". I saw the heavenly Father very far from me but I had a foretaste of his heavenly presence. I went on meditating for about five hours. When I came back into the world of senses I felt that a change had happened in me. I was not the same person as before. My senses and intellect could not grasp what I experienced. But gradually I could see the hidden power within me was growing. This experience opened a new orientation in my life. I began to know more about myself in relation with the cosmos and with Jesus. After many years of Yogic meditation and study of the Bible and Hindu Scriptures with the help of my Guru and other Spiritual teachers, I now understand at least something of what I experienced. In the light of my present knowledge I would say it was an experience of the Cosmic Christ's body. "My body became bigger and bigger" that is a process of going from one level of consciousness to an other — from my individual consciousness to the Cosmic Consciousness. In the Cosmic Consciousness I experienced the whole cosmos as my body. My body is Jesus Christ's body and my blood is Jesus Christ's blood, that is, it was an experience of the Cosmic Body of Christ. I passed from Cosmic Consciousness to Cosmic Christ Consciousness, where I was on the level of consciousness as a member of the Cosmic Body of Christ. Or I would say I was taken from my individual body consciousness to the Cosmic Christ Body Consciousness.

2. *The Name of Jesus Is More Powerful than the Wild Elephant*

In 1970 after my Brahmachariya diksha, that is the first profession, I went to Sabrimala forest in Kerala and lived there forty days in prayer and fasting with one meal a day. In the forest there was a 'sataram' (inn) where I was staying alone.

One day after midnight a wild elephant came to the place where I was sleeping and put its trunk through the window. It could easily break through and come in. Suddenly I got up and went to the other side of the room about ten feet away from the elephant. I started singing loudly the Name of Jesus 'Om Nama Christaya' (adoration to Christ). A fear arose in me, but with all my heart and soul and strength I went on singing. There was no one else to help me; so I naturally put all my trust in Jesus Christ. I surrendered myself to him. Suddenly an inner voice told me, if Jesus Christ is so close to me, closer than myself, if my body is Jesus Christ's body and my blood is Jesus Christ's blood, then why to fear? He is more powerful than the elephant. The elephant just remained where it was, putting its trunk through the window. Then I realized that it was enjoying my singing. After fifteen minutes it went away and again came back after some time and remained for some more time listening to my singing and then it went away. The whole night I did not sleep but sang the Name of Jesus. I experienced that the Name of God is more powerful than the elephant. Once we put all our trust in Jesus Christ and surrender to him and call his Name with all our hearts and with all our strength, he will awaken us to his consciousness. He is so close to us, closer than we are to ourselves. I spent forty days in the forest singing the Name of Jesus. 'Om Nama Christaya'. The animals, birds, rocks, the wind, the streams, rivers, fish, the mountains and valleys sang with me, 'Om Nama Christaya'. And I felt the whole humanity, the whole creation singing with me, 'Om Nama Christaya'.

3. *What Happens to Our Consciousness while Singing Om Nama Christaya'*

I know that Christ is so close to me, closer than myself, but it is an intellectual knowledge. Either somebody told me that Christ is within me or I read it in the Bible. It is the experience of St. Paul where he says "It is not I who live but Christ who lives in me". It is not my experience. I believe that Christ is within me but that is not enough. I want to experience that Christ is so close to me, closer than myself is close to me, beyond thoughts, words, concepts, ideas. In order to grow into this experience of Christ we sing his Name "Om Nama Christaya".

Now what happens when I sing loudly 'Om Nama Christaya', with all my heart and mind and strength? What happens to my consciousness? When I call Christ by Name, I am in the state of individual body consciousness or 'I' consciousness. I am sitting here and Christ is there. I feel that he is very far from me though I know he is so close to me. I experience the distance because I am in the individual body consciousness. That is why I call him loudly by name. What exactly is this individual body consciousness? This state of consciousness is conditioned by time, matter and space; everything is seen through the senses, everything is seen as separate (dvaitam). In this state of individual body consciousness where is God? He is very far from me. Where is Christ? He is very far from me. God and myself, Christ and myself, God and man, God and the world, myself and the world, myself and other men are all far apart. The mere fact that we have to call him loudly by Name 'Om Nama Christaya', shows that Christ is very far from us. Then what happens when I call him hundreds of times? What happens when I call a person loudly several times? Certainly he will come to me. If he does not come, I will go there because I feel his absence and need his presence. Similarly when I call Christ by Name several times, he will certainly come to me, or I will be drawn towards him. When I come to the realization of my sinfulness or impurities and the holiness of Jesus, I feel the distance between us. But when I call him hundreds and hundreds of times with my heart and strength with full trust in him surely he will come to me.

When a person is far from me I will call him loudly and when he is nearer I will call him more softly. Similarly I start singing the Name, 'Om Nama Christaya', when the chanting becomes softer and softer it is a sign that Christ is coming closer to me or I am drawn closer to Christ. In my consciousness the distance between myself and Christ gradually decreases. I get into a rhythmic movement of mental singing with the rhythmic movement of my breathing in and out. That is 'Mantra' (mental repetitions of the sacred name). The movement of the breath and the mind work together.

While I do the mental repetition, I am still in the individual body consciousness. The concentration is inside me and the awareness is that Christ is inside me, but still I call him mentally because we are not one. In the first state when I started singing vocally, Christ was outside me; when I start singing mentally he is inside my body. Gradually the mental repetition stops by itself and that is the sign that I am taken into Christ Consciousness. In this state of consciousness I know him and he knows me. My mind is one with his mind. My individual body consciousness becomes one with his consciousness and I enter into a personal relationship with

Christ. Here I am no more experiencing him through name. I had to die in order to give birth to the Christ Consciousness within me. This does not mean that I disappear altogether, but like St. Paul, I can say Christ lives in me.

Once I am in Christ Consciousness I begin to experience God the way Jesus did. I begin to pray the way Jesus was praying. It is the unique experience of Jesus that God is his Father. In fact in the history of various religious experiences we won't find a person who went so deeply into the heart of God and experienced him as a Father as Jesus did. Different people have different experiences of God. If you repeat the name Krishna, you will enter into Krishna Consciousness and experience God the way that Krishna did. If you repeat the Name of Christ, you will enter into Christ Consciousness and experience God in the way that Christ did. Calling Christ by Name means accepting him as our Lord and Master and allowing ourselves to be awakened by his power.

Now how was Jesus praying? His prayer was addressed to the Father. His mantra was Abba (Father in Aramaic). And Jesus taught us also to pray to the Father. Besides this Father - Son Consciousness, Jesus had the consciousness that the whole creation was his body, the whole of humanity was his body. "I am the vine, you are the branches, you are the sheep, I am the shepherd". Once I start to grow in Christ Consciousness and my mind becomes one with Christ, then I will begin to experience the whole creation as my body. My behaviour will change and become more like Christ's behaviour. I will begin to experience as St. Paul did the Mystical Body of Christ. "Christ is the head and the whole creation is his body." I am a member of the mystical body of Christ. Or I may experience the way St. John recorded the experience of Jesus: "I and the

Father are one." "The Father is in me and I am in the Father." "Father, may they all be one in us, as you are in me and I in you." My experience of God and the world will be like that of Jesus. I grow into the consciousness of God in and through Christ Consciousness by repeating the mantra, 'Om Nama Christaya'. hundreds and hundreds of times.

4. *First Technique of Meditation with Singing the Mantra 'Om Nama Christaya'*

Sit in a steady and pleasant posture — in Sanskrit 'Stira Sukha Asana'. Keep the eyes closed and become aware of the breathing, where the breath comes from and where it goes. Become aware of the air moving in and out through the nostrils. Practice some deep breathing, inhaling and exhaling six times. Gradually become more and more aware of your concentration. It will bring you to the awareness of yourself, your breath, your body, your mind. Through this breathing you come to the presence of your own self.

After about five minutes with all your heart and mind and strength focused on Jesus Christ our Lord and Master, ask him to awaken you from your sleep state or ego-centered state. The Master, the Lord himself, gives the power to the seeker to call him by Name. Now you can sing the Holy Name 'Om Nama Christaya'. Repeat this mantra vocally for about five minutes. Then gradually let the voice become softer and softer until it dies into your own body. The mouth now closes and the repetition continues in the heart. Keep up the mental repetition of the mantra for about five minutes.

There should be complete stillness of the entire body; do not move any part, even your little finger. Keep the whole body and mind relaxed. Now for the next five minutes just sit in stillness and experience what is happening within you. Become aware of your body outside and inside, become aware of the mind. After twenty-five minutes of meditation, stretch out your legs and relax or get up and walk for five minutes, but keep silence. If you have an hour at your disposal for meditation, repeat the same method for another thirty minutes. You must meditate this way for a minimum of eight hours. The meditation can be done within one, two or three days, or even eight days by meditating one hour a day. During the eight days you can either meditate for half an hour each morning and evening or at any convenient time of the day or night, the most auspicious time being sunrise and sunset. If you are going to do the eight hours of meditation within one day, then it should be done under the guidance of a teacher. In this case after each hour of meditation there should be an interval of at least half an hour.

While repeating the mantra vocally or mentally, if any thoughts or sounds come in, I welcome them and integrate them with the singing. The vibration of the mantra has the power to absorb all thoughts and sounds. These become part of the mantra and part of me. They are no more distracting, because in this consciousness everything is part of me, part of my body. I am aware of everything around me and in me but I will be able to get through the level of the senses and grow in Christ Consciousness, if I undergo the experience of death through total detachment from my individual body consciousness and whatever belongs to that level.

Instead of the mantra 'Om Nama Christaya,' one can choose the mantra 'Sri Yeshu Jai Yeshu Jai Jai Abba Om' or 'Yeshu Yeshu Jai Jai Abba' (glory to Jesus, glory to the Father) or the mantra 'Yeshu Yeshu Yeshuve' (Jesus, Jesus, Jesus).

PART II

YESHU ABBA CONSCIOUSNESS THROUGH CONSCIOUS BREATHING

1 Why Conscious Breathing Is So Important for Yogic Meditation.

2 How God's Spirit Is Revealed to Us through the Breath.

3 Yogic Experience of God's Self Revelation of the Trinitarian Life through the Theology of the Breath.

4 Breathing Exercise before Meditation.

5 Second Technique of Meditation; Breathing the Maha Mantra Yē and Ā.

PART II

YESHU ABBA CONSCIOUSNESS THROUGH CONSCIOUS BREATHING

1. *Why Conscious Breathing Is So Important for Yogic Meditation*

If there is an inner life of God then certainly that life is manifested in me, and surely I will be able to experience God's divine life within me. This divine life is communicated to me through the natural life movement. This is the manifestation of the life of God. Movement is one of the most obvious signs of life, and breathing (prana and apana) is a visible form of this movement. So to experience the inner life of God you first experience the natural life through the help of conscious breathing. When you become aware of where the breath comes from and where it goes, you realize that this movement comes not from your own body but from outside of it. The more you follow the breath and become one with it, the more you realize that it comes from that source from where you received your life. It is man's experience that his source of life is from God. That means that breathing in is the way in which we receive the life of God and breathing out is the way that God draws us towards him in order to give us his life. While breathing out we move towards God to receive the breath and while breathing in God moves towards us to give his life. Breathing in and breathing out is the movement from God to me and me to God. It is a natural external sign of the eternal life of God present in me. This is why conscious breathing is so important for yogic experience of the inner life of God. We know that the Eastern Fathers used to repeat the 'Jesus Prayer' with the breathing. Hindus repeat a mantra with the breathing and the Hindu yogis have developed various elaborate meditation techniques with controlled breathing (Pranayama).

2. *How God's Spirit Is Revealed to Us through the Breath*

"God has revealed Himself to us through the Spirit. The Spirit searches everything even the depths of God. What person knows a man's thoughts except the spirit of man which is in him? So also no-one comprehends the thoughts of God except the Spirit of God. Now we have received not the spirit of the world, but the Spirit which is from God, that we may understand the gifts bestowed on us by God. And we impart this in words not taught by human wisdom but taught by the Spirit, interpreting spiritual truths to those who possess the Spirit." (I Corinthians 2:10-13). Man with his intellect, mind and senses or with reasoning and thinking cannot understand God. Only the Spirit of God can get into the depths of God.

He has given that Spirit to each one of us, it is within us and with the help of this Spirit we will be able to get in to the depth of God and experience him. That means the scientific mind of man must recognize the power of the Spirit within us.

How did we get the idea of the Spirit? Somebody might have told us that there is Spirit. Perhaps a priest told us in his sermon. How did the priest get the idea? He learned from the scriptures. Then how did the Bible get it? Through the prophets. How does God communicate his Spirit to the prophets? He communicates his Spirit through natural means because man is conditioned by time, matter and space. The first sentence of Genesis tells us how. "In the beginning God's Spirit moved over the water like a wind" (Gen 1:2). At the creation we are told that "God breathed into the nostrils of man and man became a living soul" (Gen 2:2). Again God revealed himself to Elijah the prophet by a gentle breeze (I King 19:12) "Christ breathed his Spirit over the apostles" (John 20:22). The Holy Spirit came at Pentecost "like a strong wind" (Acts 2:2). "Jesus cried on the Cross, Father into thy hands I commend my Spirit. And having said this he breathed his last" (Luke 23:46). To give up the spirit into the hands of God is to emit one's final breath and at the same time to surrender to God your most precious possession, your very being. The spirit is a force inseparable from breath and life. "And her spirit returned and she got up at once" (Luke 8:55). It is said in the Psalms "you send forth your breath, they (animals) are created, and you will renew the face of the earth" (Psalm 104:130). This text is able to call forth with equal appropriateness the cosmic image of the divine breath whose rhythm rules the changes of the seasons and the pouring out of the Holy Spirit verifying the human hearts.

In every language — Hebrew 'ruah', Greek 'Pneuma', Latin 'spiritus', Sanskrit 'prana' — there is a common name borrowed from the natural phenomena of wind and air signifying supernatural power. From these quotations we can see that God communicated his Spirit through the natural vital force, the breath. Air is the closest element by which we can understand the Spirit. It is close to us, inside us, all around us. It is the vital force that keeps us alive. We cannot see it but we experience it and live by it. Spirit too is close to us, all around us. It is the vital force that keeps us alive. We cannot see it but we experience it and live by it. While breath is the natural vital force, Spirit is the eternal vital force. The natural vital force is the way through which the eternal vital force is communicated to me. Since the Spirit of God is inseparable from the breath, we use the breath as a means to experience the indwelling presence of the Holy Spirit. Awakened by the Holy Spirit and filled with its power you will be able to enter into the heart of God. So conscious breathing is one of the means to come in contact with the Spirit and through the Spirit the understanding of God. This breathing will gradually lead a person to the deep silence beyond the senses and its activities, beyond the reasoning of the intellect where you will be able to listen to the subtle inner voice of the Spirit of God.

3. *Yogic Experience of God's Self Revelation of the Trinitarian Life through the Theology of the Breath*

When God wanted to share his inner life, his Spirit moved from within him. "In the beginning. . . . the Spirit of God moved over the water (like a wind)". This is the first act of creation, the first expression of God's self-giving. The movement of the Spirit of God is expressed as the Breath of God. He breathes out his Spirit and when the Spirit moves there is vibration, producing the subtle voice of God. From this subtle voice the Word comes forth. "And God said, let there be light". This is the beginning of creation which reaches its climax when God breathed into the nostrils of man the breath of life. "The Lord God formed man from the dust of the ground and breathed into his nostrils the breath of life, and man became a living being." "God created everything by his Spirit, his Breath, and by his Word." The life-giving Spirit of God through the Breath in the form of the Word gave birth to the whole creation, to the whole humanity, and finally to Jesus Christ. It is man's experience of the inner life of God the supernatural power, the salvific work of God, which is expressed through the mythological symbolism of breath in the story of Genesis. The creation narrative is a mythological story through which man's experience of the supernatural power of God's salvific work from chaos to cosmos is experienced.

Imagine that I am sitting in front of you. I want to give myself fully to you. But if I try to give myself to you like this you will not be able to accept me. Still the love within me urges me to give myself to you in such a way that you can receive me. What happens when I talk to you? I breathe out through the mouth and the words are heard. The words are produced through the vibration. From this you get a certain knowledge of me. This is the way I give myself to you, through my breath.

This will help us to understand the way God gives himself to us. If he comes to me as he is, I will not be able to receive or understand him. He is too great, too powerful. "Man cannot see God and live." "Moses saw only the back of God". I am still conditioned by body, mind and senses and their limitations, time, matter and space and as long as I am subject to these factors I will not be able to understand God. But God wants to share his inner life with us so he raises us to the state where he is by the power of his Word. "In the Beginning was the Word, and the Word was with God, and the Word was God." "All things were made through him." "In him was life, and the life was the light of man." "And the Word was made flesh and dwelt among us." "No one has ever seen God, only the Son, who is in the bosom of the Father, he has made him known."

The prologue of St. John's Gospel and the creation narrative will both help us to understand the theology of breath. When God breathed out his Spirit, the Word was heard. The Word stands for God. From the Word the Spirit brings forth the whole creation. Everything exists in the Word, everything comes forth from the Word. As we read in Genesis, God spoke and everything came into existence, and in St. John we read all things were made in and through the Word of God.

Now this Word in whom the whole creation and the whole humanity is present, who was with God in the beginning and who was God, incarnates by the power of the Holy Spirit and is called Jesus of Nazareth. By his death and resurrection he was raised as the Lord of the Universe. He is the Son of God. He is the image of God. "He who sees me sees the Father." He is the self-manifestation of God and the light and life of man. St. Paul experienced him as the Cosmic Man. "Christ is the head and the whole creation his body." "Things on earth and things in heaven gathered together in unity in Christ". The

Risen Lord Jesus Christ, the Cosmic Man, is the Breath of God in whom the whole creation is present, in whom the whole humanity is present. This is the evolution of God's revelation. The Cosmic Man, Jesus Christ, whose body is the whole creation and who is the image and likeness of God, shares the inner life of God. Only someone who is like God can share the divine life of God.

Jesus Christ, the Cosmic Man, fulfilled God's purpose of sharing the divine life. As we are members of the Mystical Body of Christ we also will be able to share the inner life of God. The evolution of God's revelation is still in the process of its growth. The revelation of God from the beginning of the creation until the Risen Lord Jesus Christ who is seated in the bosom of God the Father has to be taken as one event in its past, present and future. This must be realized in man and experienced consciously. Jesus Christ fully experienced this mystery and we as members of his Cosmic Body must do the same. We do this in and through Jesus Christ.

We saw already the movement of God's self-giving revelation to share his inner life. That is, God breathes out himself through the breath. The Breath of God stands for God himself as Spirit. When God's Spirit moved from within him as Breath the Word came forth. From the Word the whole creation came forth, and finally the Word became flesh as Jesus Christ the Son of God. Now Jesus is the Risen Lord who dwells everywhere, but I cannot see him or understand him. He is abstract. He is very far away. So the Risen Lord comes to me through the Spirit. Jesus told the apostles when he was taken to the Father from the sight of man: "I will send you the Holy Spirit."

But still if the Spirit comes to us as pure spirit we will not be able to understand or receive it. So the Spirit comes to us through the Breath. The Holy Spirit comes at Pentacost "like a stormy wind". "Christ breathed his Spirit over the apostles". We already know what breath is. It is the vital force that sustains our natural life. I cannot see it but I can experience it. Breath is the closest element through which we can identify the Spirit.

The movement of God's self-giving revelation in the logical order is as follows:

> God the Father → Spirit → Breath → Word → creation headed by man → Jesus of Nazareth → Risen Lord Jesus Christ the Cosmic Man → Holy Spirit → Breath → Myself

This is the way that God comes to me, the movement from God to me. The revelation of God to man.

The Breath of God returns to the one who sent it not with empty hands but with full fruit. The Holy Spirit, the Spirit of my master, enters within me and awakens me from my lower state of consciousness, my individual body consciousness. This is the earth-centered state, ego-centered state, self-centered state, ignorant state and sleep state. Jesus Christ awakens me from my sinful state of disharmony and chaos and brings me into the awareness of his own consciousness.

In response to God's self-giving revelation I receive with an open heart the Breath of God and allow myself to be drawn towards God. The Breath of God is in everything that comes forth from God and that is the Risen Lord Jesus Christ the Cosmic Man — in one word Yeshu. I breathe in, everything, in and through Yeshu and breathe out myself with Yeshu to the Father. Through Yeshu-Consciousness I enter into Father-Consciousness. Through Jesus Christ we share the sonship of

God. That means through the Consciousness of Christ, we as the children of God breathe in the Father through the Spirit and breathe out ourselves to the Father through the same Spirit. We with our limited power alone will not be able to breathe out and give ourselves to God because we are too much conditioned by our ego-centered state.

The responsive movement of God's self-giving revelation is the movement from me to God. In the logical order it is as follows:

Myself → Breath → Holy Spirit → Risen Lord Jesus Christ the Cosmic Man → Jesus of Nazareth → Creation headed by man → Word → Breath → Holy Spirit → God the Father

The mantra Yeshu expresses the movement from the Father to me through the Son Jesus as I breathe in. The mantra Abba expresses the movement from me to the Father through the Son Jesus as I breathe out. The mantra must be as short as possible and as fluent as the breathing. So we cut short the name Yeshu to Yē and the rest of the name 'shu' is silent. In the same way we use for the name Abba Ā and the rest of the name 'bba' is silent. God the Father is continuously moving towards me. When there is a movement, vibration is produced and the vibration is expressed as Yē. When God the Father draws me towards Him there is a vibration and this vibration is expressed as A. Thus we get the mantra Yē and Ā. There is a deeper reason why the mantra becomes shorter. When I become very close to a person I normally will not call that person by his full name but rather call him with just part of the name. The best example is that of husband and wife. In their deep relationship the husband will not call the wife by her full name and the wife will not call the husband by his full name. They will use only a part, or sometimes be able to communicate with each other without any names. This is what happens when we enter into the personal relationship with each other without any names. This is what happens when we enter into the personal relationship with Yeshu and Abba. The name becomes shorter and shorter until finally we transcend the name and enter into the silence of the Yeshu Abba Consciousness.

4. *Breathing Exercise before Meditation*

Sit in your stira sukhasana, steady and pleasant posture, for meditation. If you are not able to sit comfortably in 'sukhasana' easy squatting, 'Ardhapadmasana' half lotus or 'Padmasana' full lotus, then sit in 'Vajrasana' (sitting on the open heels) for this breathing exercise. One must master Vibhaga Pranayama (sectional breathing) and Mahat Yoga Pranayama (Complete breathing) before starting the meditation on the Maha Mantra Yē and Ā.

VIBHAGA PRANAYAMA

a. Abdominal Breathing

To control the lower lobes of the lungs, place hands on the diaphragm region. Breathe deeply in and out, expanding the abdomen with inhalation and contracting the abdomen with exhalation. The hands should move with the breathing, indicating that the air is filling the lowest part of the lungs.Timing 3:3 seconds or 6:6 seconds. After 3 to 6 rounds of this type of breathing, move the hands to the outside of the lower rib cage and feel that the air is filling the sides of the lower lungs. Repeat 3 to 6 rounds.

Turn the hands around to the back, so that the fingers are pointing towards the spine and concentrate on filling the back section of the lower lungs for 3 to 6 rounds.

b. Mid-chest Breathing

For the control of the breath in the middle area of the lungs, place both hands flat on the chest. Breathe deeply in and out so that the hands move apart with inhalation and back together with exhalation. Breathe for 3 to 6 rounds.

Now place the hands on the outside middle area of the ribs and breathe deeply for 3 to 6 rounds, the ribs should act like accordion (sideways) to allow for the breath to fill this area.

Place the hands as far around the back, middle area as possible, fingers pointing towards the spine and concentrate the breathing to this area for 3 to 6 rounds.

c. High-chest Breathing

To control the high chest area of the lungs, place both hands on the upper chest just below the collar bone. Breathe deeply in and out so that the hands are raised by the inhalation and lowered by the exhalation. Keep the shoulders relaxed.

After 3 to 6 rounds move the hands to the hips so that the armpits are unobstructed and concentrate on the side high lobes of the lungs so that the breathing is felt in the area of the armpits. Do 3 to 6 rounds.

Raise the hands over the shoulders and place the palms on the back high area of the lungs. Concentrate the mind on breathing in this area for 3 to 6 rounds.

MAHAT YOGA PRANAYAMA

Place the right hand on the abdomen, the other palm on the mid-chest area. While breathing deeply fill the abdomen first, then the mid-chest and then the upper chest using the right hand as a guide when breathing into each section. Inhale 2 seconds to abdomen, 2 seconds to mid-chest, 2 seconds to high chest. Retain for 6 seconds. Exhale first from the abdomen for 2 seconds, mid-chest for 2 seconds, high chest for 2 seconds. So the timing is 6:6:6: inhalation, retention, exhalation. After several days of practice add 6 seconds of suspension (holding with no breath).

5. *Second Technique of Meditation; Breathing the Maha Mantra Yē and Ā*

Become aware of the breathing. Follow its movement. Once you become aware of the incoming breath you will feel the air passing through the nostrils and going into the lungs and in the same way the out-going breath passes out through the nostrils into the atmosphere. If you follow the breath more closely you will find where it comes from and where it goes and finally experience the ultimate source of the air which is from God from whom we receive life. So, breathing in begins from God and breathing out ends in God. Concentration begins while breathing in on that ultimate reality behind the atmosphere and then as the air passes through the nose, concentrate on the entrance of the nostrils and follow the air passing into the lower part of the lungs while the abdomen expands, then the mid-chest, then the upper chest. While breathing out begin the concentration from the abdomen area which is the ground of your being, following the air while the abdomen contracts first, then the mid-chest, then the upper chest and finally following the air passing out the nostrils to the atmosphere and ending in that ultimate reality beyond.

The flow of concentration can be shown like this. While breathing in from God — atmosphere — entrance of nostrils — abdomen area — mid-chest — upper chest. While breathing out from the Abdomen — mid-chest — upper chest —entrance of the nostrils — atmosphere — God. While breathing keep the awareness that we are breathing in the Breath of God. God's own self which is coming to me through the prana in the air and while breathing out I give myself from the very ground of my being to God. This whole movement from God to me and from me to God is expressed through the Maha Mantra (the great breathing) Yē and Ā.

Listen to the vibration, the subtle voice, while breathing in and out. Certain vibrations are produced during breathing. If we listen attentively with full concentration we will be able to hear the sound Yē while inhaling and Ā while exhaling. Start mental repetition of these sounds while breathing in and out. Integrate the mantra with the vibration of the breathing. The mind, the awareness, the mantra, the breath and the vibration must work together as one movement. I must be fully present with all my heart, mind and strength.

Sum up all our ideas and thoughts about God, world and man into this one name, Yeshu and Abba. In order to understand the person Yeshu-Abba we study scripture. All the intellectual studies and reflections must be done before the meditation. Once the Yogic meditation proper begins there should be less and less intellectual reflections. In Yogic meditation we allow ourselves to enter into the personal relationship with God beyond thoughts, words and name. We allow ourselves to experience God, the world and men in our own body in the silence of intellect, mind and senses.

Concentrate on the mantra Yē and Ā while breathing in and out. Gradually one will be taken into a deep silence where breath itself becomes the mantra. That means one will transcend the mantra Yē and Ā but still the breathing in and out continues. In this deep silence one experiences the movement from God to man and man to God from Father to Son and Son to Father. The total self-giving movement from God the Father to me in and through Yeshu and from me to the Father in and through Abba. Here one enters into the Father-Son relationship and experiences the Trinitarian life of God. In this state of Yeshu Abba Consciousness one allows oneself to be moved by the movement of the Spirit which is experienced and expressed through the conscious breathing. Allow oneself to remain in this movement consciously and experience the inner life of God the way it manifests.

In the beginning do this meditation for about twenty minutes. Gradually increase the time.

PART III

PRATHYAHARA — WITHDRAWAL
How to Face Various Types of Obstacles in Meditation

PART III

PRATHYAHARA — WITHDRAWAL
How to Face Various Types of Obstacles in Meditation

Introduction

In Yogic meditation in order to transcend the individual body consciousness, which is conditioned by the intellect, the senses and their activities — motions, feelings, desires and thoughts — and to get into the deep silence in the stillness of the mind, we concentrate with all our hearts, minds and strength on the mantra Yē and Ā while inhaling and exhaling. In the process of this meditation we have to face lots of distractions. The moment we begin the concentration the mind starts wandering into various objects. The yogic control of the mind and the senses is called in 'Prathyahara' withdrawal, the fifth step of Raja Yoga. There are two ways of understanding the practising Prathyahara, or withdrawal. One is a negative approach and the other is positive.

1. *The Negative Approach for Withdrawal and Its Defect*

Withdraw the senses from the sense objects to inside the center of our being. The traditional example is the Tortoise. When it senses any disturbance, it withdraws the head, tail and legs into the hard shell and remains inside without knowing what is happening outside. When I follow this type of withdrawal, I have to face two kinds of distractions — one from inside and the other from outside. For example I am sitting for meditation. The people and the world are around me. I close my eyes from the people who are in front of me in order to concentrate in the center of my being. For a few minutes I may succeed to concentrate. After that a desire arises in me to open my eyes and look at the people. And also the people who are sitting in front of me are looking at me. They are communicating something to me. Here I am creating distractions. The tension is from inside as well as from outside objects. The senses always want the sense objects and they are meant for that. When I close my eyes from the sense objects I am doing violence to my eyes. My eyes want to see. I close my eyes so that I may not see. Here I am not fulfilling the duty of the senses.

Another example: I am sitting in meditation when suddenly I hear some noise around me. Immediately I react and avoid the noise. I try not to hear the noise. I try to withdraw myself from the sense of hearing. But the more I try to avoid the noise, the more the tension increases in me. The noise continues to disturb me. I create a negative attitude towards the noise. Since the noise is from an outside object I cannot stop it. The noise goes on disturbing me. Even if I succeed in concentration and am able to enter into silence, when I come back to the senses I will have still a negative attitude towards the noise. That means the tension will remain in me. This type of negative withdrawal of the senses from the sense objects is very much related to our own religious understanding of God, man and the world. In our old spirituality we were taught that there are three enemies of our spiritual life. I was taught in my catechism that the world, the flesh and the devil are the three enemies of spiritual life. If I want to grow in spiritual life I must continuously fight against these enemies. That means in meditation I must withdraw my senses from the world, from the flesh and from the devil. In this view the whole world around me, that means the whole humanity, is an enemy for my spiritual life and I must withdraw the senses from the world, from the people, in order to turn inside to the center of my being, to be alone with God who is within me. Here the world and the people have nothing to do with my spiritual life. They are my enemies. Not only the world and the people but my own flesh must be regarded as an enemy in order to free the soul from the body. This comes from the religious understanding that the body is impure and when we die the soul is separated from the body and the soul alone goes to God. And finally the devil is an enemy. What else is there under heaven? Whatever God created is an enemy for my spiritual life and I must withdraw from them all. The world, the flesh and the devil have nothing to do with my spiritual life. The cloistered religious life is very much influenced by this type of spirituality. I remember in the beginning of my monastic life. I was told not to talk to the guests, because they are coming from the world and any association with them may cause temptation or disturbance in spiritual life.

Once I was attending a seminar with a Benedictine nun.

She was the superior of her convent. She told me, 'Brother! I don't like going out at all for seminars or even to the town. First of all I miss the divine office. More than that I feel myself like a fish out of water, I get lost in the world.' This type of negative spirituality is found not only in Christianity and Hinduism but in all religions. In the scriptures too we find this type of spirituality. Jesus uses this type of language, when he says "When you pray go to your room and close the door and pray to your Father." "If you want to follow me, you must hate your father and mother." "Unless you deny yourself you cannot be my disciple." People took these teachings literally and followed them.

Running away from the world to a convent and remaining inside the walls without knowing what is happening in the world outside the convent walls or going into the desert or to the caves in the forest are very much influenced by this negative religious spirituality which holds that the world, the flesh and the devil are the three enemies of the spiritual life. According to this I must be alone with God. All the rest is an obstacle to being alone with God.

THE DEFECT OF THIS NEGATIVE WITHDRAWAL

I gradually developed a kind of negative attitude or consciousness in me towards everything. This type of negative attitude was seen very much in the people who lived in the cloistered convents, monasteries, caves and desert places. If I hold these negative attitudes towards men and the world I will find it extremely difficult to live in this world. I will be unfit for the world. I will not be able to face people. I will be always in a kind of tension. It will prevent me seeing good in anything.

2. *The Positive Approach for Withdrawal and Its Effect*

Sit in meditation posture. Become aware of the objects outside. Keep the senses alert. Get into the sense objects through the senses and bring the sense objects also with the senses inside the center of your being. Here I am fulfilling the duty of the senses. Now I have the experience that everything is within me and nothing outside of me to disturb. The senses brought everything into me and made me feel that everything is part of me. The technique is breathing in everything, in and through Yeshu. Gradually I enter into the awareness that Jesus is within me and I in him. Things on earth and things in heaven are gathered together in unity. What is the withdrawal here? In the first state I am seeing everything through my senses. Here there is a type of withdrawal. I am no more seeing things as I was seeing before. In the first state where there is no withdrawal, I see things through my senses as outside of me. That is the state of the individual body consciousness, that is, I and the objects are two (dividam). In this state the senses remain with the sense objects on the level of sense activities, emotions, feelings, desires, thoughts, etc. The actual positive withdrawal is from this state of sense activity to the stillness of the senses, where the senses and the sense objects are experienced as 'not two'. So the particularity of the positive withdrawal is that in this state of consciousness one experiences the stillness of the mind and senses not through cutting away the senses from the sense objects but through the presence of the sense objects with the senses in the mind. So the withdrawal in its deepest sense is not that I separate myself from other beings but rather that I enter into the one body consciousness or Cosmic Consciousness.

One can experience two kinds of Prathyahara. One is when our mind and senses are in stillness. The other is when our mind and senses are active as well as conditioned by the lower state of consciousness. In this state the mind and the sense get lost in the sense objects and remain immersed in the pleasures of the senses, emotions, feelings, desires and thoughts. And in this state one believes this is everything and that there is nothing beyond. Here the man, the ego, is the center, not God.

THE EFFECT OF THE POSITIVE WITHDRAWAL

After this kind of Prathyahara when I open my eyes, when I come out of the meditation, I will be able to relate myself to others. The love and concern for others will flow spontaneously. I will still have the consciousness that everything around me is part of me. The mountains and trees, rivers and streams, grass and flowers, animals, birds and men, the whole world is part of me and I need them and they need me. I will feel at home everywhere; in a noisy city as well as in the countryside.

3. *Healing of Hatred and Enmity*

I had an enemy. I really hated him and he hated me. In the depth of my heart I had always an anger towards him. I used to quarrel with him very often. Since I did not like him, any little thing was enough to cause an upset. I found it extremely difficult to understand him and accept him. I could not trust him for anything. One day I had a real fight with him and I lost control of myself and said many wounding words to him.

Our enmity became worse. For many days both of us went on without talking to each other. Our spiritual Father used to call us together whenever any quarrel arose. He told us about Christian charity and forgiveness. And in fact he succeeded to a certain extent in reconciling us. For a few days we would be able to go peacefully. But after a week or two again something would happen and our relationship would become worse than before. That means no fundamental change took place in us. On one level of Consciousness we might have been able to understand each other but on a deeper level of Consciousness the wounds of hatred and anger remained.

During the day I may have a quarrel with my brother. In the evening I go to the church for meditation. I am really upset. Sometimes in this situation I do not have any interest in meditation or prayer. Sometimes I am unable to meditate. If I do meditate then it is as follows: I take the Bible and find the passage: "Love your enemy as yourself." I close the book and start reflecting on this great teaching of Jesus. After the reflection, I pray to Jesus: "Pardon me, put a new heart in me, take away the hatred, enmity and anger from me. Give me, Jesus, a loving heart. Jesus be with me always." And finally I make a resolution, Tomorrow even if my enemy says something against me I will not react; I will not get angry with him; I will love him; I will look at him and smile. With this resolution I conclude the meditation. The next day in the morning I renew the intention. I will not react, even if he says something against me; I will love him. During the day also I recall to my mind the resolution which I made during the meditation and the Mass. My enemy and I are living together. We belong to the same community. We are working together every day. Now during the work, he says something which hurts me very much and suddenly I get angry with him. I react immediately. Our enmity becomes worse than yesterday. I do not want to get angry with him but I get angry. I cannot control my feelings and emotions.

Afterwards, when I come back to my room, I say to myself, what is the use of meditating like this and going for Mass every day? There is no change taking place in me. I am becoming worse day by day. Hatred and anger between me and my enemy are increasing day by day. I find it extremely difficult to face him and live with him.

I try to analyse my prayer. I took the Bible. I opened it and found the passage, "Love your enemy." I reflected on it. I asked Jesus to put a new heart in me. I made the intellectual resolution that even if my enemy said something against me I would not react. I would love him, I would smile at him. Everything I did myself in my head. Next day when the event took place, I did not want to get angry but I got angry. Everything in this prayer I did myself intellectually by reasoning: This is not really prayer. Prayer must be a total transformation of the whole person. In deep prayer it is not I who pray but I allow the Spirit to pray with his own language. In this prayer the ego was predominantly active. The total humility was not there. This type of intellectual prayer very often does not make much change in the attitude of the person. To a certain extent an intellectual change may take place. When I was reading and reflecting on the scripture passage, "Love your enemy as yourself" my head was fully involved. When the event took place, at that particular moment the head was not present, the rest of my body was involved — I would say below the neck. The intellect and reason could not do anything or they were absent at that moment. Intellectually by reasoning I didn't want to get angry but I got angry. What is anger? Anger is a kind of tension. The external event awakened the deep-rooted anger from my subconscious and my nervous system manifested it. When I was praying intellectually this anger towards my enemy was sleeping in my subconscience or it was suppressed and kept in the subconscious. The ordinary type of prayer and reflection does not deal with the deep-rooted anger in the subconscious, in the depth of our heart. That means that when I was praying, the tension was not released. So when the event took place I could not control my tension and my nervous system was very weak and I got angry and shouted at him and I became very violent and forgot myself, and in words and action I wounded my enemy. We became ten times higher enemies. When a quarrel takes place the intellect and reason play very little part compared to the emotions and feelings which are awakened from the subconscious.

When I was praying, one part of my person was involved, and when the event took place the other part of the person was involved. In real prayer the whole person will be involved and a transformation of the whole person will take place. If the wound of anger in the depth of my heart was healed while I was praying, then when the event took place I would not have got angry with him but rather I would have smiled at him.

WHEN I WAS PRAYING MY ENEMY HAD NOTHING TO DO WITH ME AND WHEN THE EVENT TOOK PLACE I HAD TO ENCOUNTER HIM

For prayer and meditation I went alone and sat in a quiet place. I wanted to be alone with God. My enemy had nothing to do with my prayer. He was not present with me to pray. I prayed to Jesus and asked grace from him. I withdrew myself from the people, from the world, in this case from my enemy. After the prayer I came out of the chapel and went to work with my enemy. I had to live with him and work with him. There was no escape from it. When I encountered him during the work, I could not find Jesus in him, because he was my enemy. I did not like him. I could see only hatred and aggression. When I was in the chapel I could see Jesus but as soon as I came out of the chapel, Jesus disappeared. When I was praying I did not need my enemy but at other times of the day I need him.

One day I was sitting on the bank of the river with a deep desire to become one with my enemy. I really wanted to get rid of this hatred within me. With all my heart and strength I concentrated on my enemy. Though I did not like him, he was always in my mind. I started breathing him in. I could not take him in. I could not keep him in my mind consciously and feel that he was part of me. When I started breathing him in, I found that I choked. I could not even breathe in. I did not like him, then how could I keep him in me? Though I wanted to get rid of the hatred in me, I found myself powerless to do so. In that case my enemy too was powerless to become one with me. We were both in a state of helplessness, unable to get rid of the hatred because we both looked at each other with an evil heart. In my powerlessness I realised the need for a powerful person, the one who looks at me and my enemy with the same heart. Here Jesus comes to help me. For Jesus my enemy and I are the same. He looks upon both of us with the same eyes. For him both of us are members of his body. Here I came to the realization that if I could enter into Yeshu

Consciousness, then in and through his consciousness I would be able to experience my enemy as part of me. At that moment Jesus demanded something from me. He was ready to unite both of us together in him but I must undergo the consequence whatever it be. The purification would take place in me and I must undergo it consciously.

I started beathing in my enemy in and through Yeshu. Here the figure of Jesus became the figure of my enemy. Jesus was coming to me as my enemy, the person whom I hate. I thought of Jesus always as someone who loves me. So far I had been told of a Jesus who is gentle, calm, affectionate and with all the positive virtues. I expected a Jesus who is full of love, joy and peace. But here Jesus came in a form contrary to my understanding and expectation. Here Jesus came to me in and through my enemy with all the negative qualities of him. But I continued to breathe in my enemy in and through Yeshu. While breathing in mentally I said Yeshu and while breathing out 'Abba'. While breathing out I gave myself to my enemy. Breathing in my enemy and breathing out myself to him. While breathing in Jesus came to me with my enemy and I became one with my enemy and Jesus. While breathing out I gave myself to my enemy in and through the Father.

I cannot go to the Father unless and until I experience my enemy as my brother and we both are members of the body of Jesus Christ and we both share the sonship with Christ. I cannot go to the Father without my brother. As we see in the book of Genesis where "the Lord said to Cain, 'where is your brother? . . . The voice of your brother's blood is crying to me from the ground' " (Gen. 4: 9-10).

For many days I went on meditating in this way, breathing in my enemy in and through Yeshu and breathing out myself to my enemy in and through the Father using the mantra Yē and Ā (Yeshu & Abba). Gradually I began to experience the consequences. My whole body began to undergo the experience of death, the pain of death. Sometimes there was terrible pain in certain parts of my body. Sometimes my throat got very dry. Sometimes my whole body started trembling. Sometimes fear came up. Like this I experienced different kinds of symptoms in my body. I could see some changes taking place in me physically, mentally, psychologically and spiritually. While breathing in my enemy there came to my conscious mind the deep-rooted hatred, anger and aggression towards my enemy. Not only that but also the negative attitude of my enemy towards me. All that he said and did against me and all that I said and did against him came to my mind. When I began to experience some silence, a lot of things from my subconscious came to my conscious mind. I sometimes even felt I was going to collapse. I really underwent an agony. My whole being underwent the pain of death. This is a state which one cannot explain but can experience. I began to discover a lot of unsolved problems which had gone to the subconscious from my younger days on. One day I experienced, "It is not I who sit but my enemy is sitting." My body and his body became one. I saw my mind in my enemy's mind and his mind in my mind. I began to see how he sees me, and how I see him. When both these visions came together in my conscious mind, while I was in deep silence, I saw my real self and my impurities. In this context I could see myself fully only in my enemy. In the fire of Yeshu-Abba Consciousness all my impurities burnt away and I began to experience my enemy and myself as the one body of Jesus. In and through Yeshu Abba Consciousness he is no more an enemy for me but he is my brother and part of my body. Deep-rooted love began to grow in me towards him. I began to experience liberation, love, joy and peace. Slowly my behaviour and attitude towards him began to change. One day after many days of meditation, I was going from the Temple to the kitchen. On the way I saw my enemy who was coming from the kitchen to the Temple. This was the time I had not been talking to him for many days. Usually I avoided him when he came towards me by choosing another path or looking down to the ground. But this time I just walked towards him, looking at his face and I smiled at him. He, too, smiled and started talking. We became good friends after that. In that moment his spirit and my spirit met in the Spirit of Jesus. In a deeper level of consciousness, I experienced, he is part of me. In and through Yeshu Abba Consciousness I began to act and move with him. I began to behave the way Jesus would behave with him. Spontaneously and naturally love began to flow from my heart.

When I was meditating I did not make any intellectual conclusion that I would love him and smile at him nor did I make any decision that even if he says something against me, I will not react. But when I met him, I just spontaneously smiled at him and loved him. That means that while I was meditating I had already undergone the experience of death and purification. The tension was released. The wounds of anger and aggression were already healed. The transformation of the whole person was taking place. The hatred was transformed into love.

To explain this one-body-consciousness, this example should help. Suppose one day I really get upset and start beating on my chest. As a consequence I hurt my chest and I begin to feel severe pain. Now I will not get angry with my hand nor will I cut off my hand because it hurt my chest. Why? Because I know that my chest and my hand are both parts of my body. I do not need to think that the hand is part of my body, I am conscious that the hand is part of my body. But I undergo the consequences of the action, that is pain, without any complaint. Because I cannot complain to myself. Consciously and willingly I cannot do any harm to myself. I must love my whole body. I will not hate myself. Similarly even if someone beats me and hurts me, I cannot react or do harm to him because I am conscious that he is part of my body. I cannot hate him. But I have to undergo the consequences of beating that is pain. This is what one body consciousness means. This is what Jesus means when he says, 'Love your enemy as yourself'. That means, it is natural for me to love myself. But if I have the consciousness that my enemy is part of my body, then I could love him as myself. In this state of one body consciousness, I experience that I am an enemy to myself because my enemy is in me, but I cannot remain enemy to myself. So, the moment I come to the awareness of this enmity within me, I undergo the pain of purification and give birth to love. That means the enmity is transformed into love. To fulfil this great teaching of Jesus, "Love your enemy as yourself," we have to grow in Cosmic Christ Body Consciousness and experience that we are members of the Mystical Body of Christ.

When Jesus was praying in the garden he had the cosmic body consciousness that the whole humanity is present in his body with all the aggression, enmity, hatred, anger, etc. At one point of his agony Jesus prayed to the Father to take away his cup from him, because the pain which he had to undergo was so severe. Jesus welcomed the hatred and anger of the people into his body and underwent the experience of purification, the pain of death. When he was beaten and mocked on the Cross, Jesus said: "Father, forgive them for they know not what they do" (Lk. 23:34). Because of his one body consciousness, that the enemy is part of his body, Jesus could not react or do any harm to his enemy, who hurt him. How far we grow in Cosmic Christ Body Consciousness, so far we grow in love and charity. Love your enemy as yourself flows from the experience of the presence of one's enemy in oneself in and through Yeshu consciousness. So breathe in your enemy and breathe out yourself to him in and through Yeshu Abba.

4. *Attachment to the Opposite Sex — Love between a Boy and a Girl, or a Man and Woman*

A young man had a girl friend. He loved her and she loved him. Now he is in the monastery and she is in her home. One day he was sitting in meditation and suddenly a desire arose in him that he wanted to see her. He wanted to have her presence. Thoughts of her were always in his mind. He could not concentrate. He could not meditate. He tried to forget her and concentrate on Jesus. For a few minutes he succeeded but afterwards the thought came back. When he began to study himself, he realised that in him there was deep-rooted love towards women. In every person there is this unquenchable thirst for the opposite sex. A man is not perfect without a woman, and woman is not perfect without a man. In man the feminine personality is lacking and in woman the masculine personality is lacking. A perfect man is male and female. So, in every man and woman there is this desire for the opposite sex and desire for union. The harmony between man and woman was there in the beginning, when God created man as male and female. This harmony has been broken but the desire for harmony is there.

What is the desire in him? He wants to see her, he needs her presence. Her absence makes him lonely. What can he do? Suppose she comes and sits near to him, is it enough? Will it satisfy his desire? No. If he touches her, embraces her, is it enough? That will not satisfy. If he yields to the desires of his senses and has sexual intercourse, will it satisfy the desire? No. His love towards her is so deep that it urges him to possess her. The love and desire are so deep that whatever he does in this physical level will not give him the ultimate fulfilment of his thirst. He wants to become 'one with her'. He wants to eat her. He wants to give his whole being to her and he wants her to give her whole being to him. They both want to become one person. So much is his love and desire for her. The normal and natural process of becoming one is marriage. In marital union the husband and wife experience to a certain extent the oneness and the presence of each other. But the physical presence is conditioned by the time, matter, space, body, mind, will, senses and emotions. Physical marriage and union is conditioned by these limitations and it will not bring the ultimate union.

So he realizes that as long as he remains in the individual body consciousness, which is conditioned by time, matter, space, body, senses and its activities, he will not be able to fulfil his desire of deep-rooted love, to become one with the other. Whatever he does on the physical level, still the distance and the absence of the other will remain. Physical closeness can unite him to a certain extent. Marriage can unite him to a certain extent. But for perfect closeness he has to transcend the physical state.

What should he do in his meditation? He closes his eyes and concentrates on the person he loves with all his heart, mind and strength. Jesus is going to come to him as this girl whom he loves so much. The figure of Jesus is her figure. It is easy for him to concentrate on this girl because she loves him and he loves her, not like the enemy. Here everything is very positive. Even if he doesn't concentrate still she is always in his mind. He starts breathing her in, in and through Yeshu and breathing out himself to her in and through Abba. While breathing in Yeshu he sees in his mind her figure, her qualities are the figure and qualities of Jesus. All the passions, desires, emotions, feelings are present in him. He goes on meditating every day for two weeks breathing her in and breathing himself out to her in and through Yeshu and Abba. Sometimes the sweet memories of the past will come up from the subconscious to the conscious mind. He goes on meditating with full awareness of what is happening to him physically, mentally, psychologically and spiritually. A lot of passions are awakened during the meditation. Sometimes they are uncontrollable. Various symptoms are experienced in the body. During the meditation there is always a tendency to remain in the lower state of consciousness, that is the state of emotions, feelings, desires, passions which is something very pleasant and good. But he is fully aware of the power of Jesus and it is he who is present in this lower state of consciousness. But he has to undergo the experience of death, this is the transcending process of lower nature to the higher nature. He has to undergo the pangs of birth in order to give birth to the love which is awakened by the power of Jesus when he enters into the depth of his being.

One day in the course of meditation he experiences that it is not he who sits here but she. His body is her body and his blood is her blood. She is so close to him — closer than he is close to himself. His mind is her mind, his feelings are her feelings. She is no more away from him. Now there is no need to open his eyes and look to see her face. He has no need to think of her to feel her presence. He has no need to smile to please her. She and he are not two. They both are one as members of the Mystical Body of Christ. In Christ they both are married and become one body as the body of Christ. This is the mystical marriage. Her spirit and his spirit meet together in the Spirit of Jesus and the marriage takes place. Jesus enters into his body with a feminine person with feminine qualities and awakens his masculine personality with the masculine qualities and the marriage between the masculine person and the feminine person takes place in Jesus.

The effect of this meditation is the experience that besides the physical body consciousness there is the psychic and spiritual body consciousness. He begins to experience the closeness of the other person, in this girl friend, without the physical closeness. Physical separation and distance are no barrier for psychic and spiritual closeness. This is what he experiences: Physically she is very far from him, but on the psychic and spiritual level she is very close to him, as close as he is to himself. The psychic and spiritual consciousness that she is present in him and that she is part of him, controls the physical consciousness and the desire to see her and to have her physical presence. So in meditation he can concentrate until he gets into deep silence beyond thoughts, words and actions and experiences the yogic harmony in Yeshu-Abba Consciousness. The thought of her becomes no more distracting, rather it awakens him into the experience of communion. It does not mean that he has no more desire to see her and have her physical presence. It is there and surely if he gets a chance he would see her and sit with her and it would bring him great joy. This awakening of the psychic and spiritual consciousness brings the physical consciousness and its activities under control, that is to say in harmony with the whole person. That means that psychic and spiritual consciousness will not allow him to be a slave of the passions and desires of the senses, of the physical body consciousness.

If he had taken a negative attitude towards her and followed a negative technique, then he would have suppressed all his feelings and the desires of the senses. Whenever the thought of her came to his mind, he would have tried to get rid of it. And finally he would come to the state that sex and sexual thoughts are evil. In meditation as well as at other times, thinking of that girl would be evil. And, finally, due to this negative approach and suppression of the feelings, he would become mentally, psychologically, as well as physically sick. And gradually he would develop a negative attitude towards women, especially girls. He would not be able to look at a girl with open heart and sincere smile. And also the women will not be free with him. They will not be able to come to him with open heart and sincere love.

5. *Mystical Marriage of the Male and Female Is the Way to Mystical Union*

Today whenever I see a woman or a girl, I breathe her in and breathe myself out to her in and through Yeshu and Abba. Not only all the women in the world I breathe in, but also all the men since masculine personality in me has to grow still. So I breathe in every human being in order to enter mystical marriage. I breathe in the animals, birds, trees, mountains and valleys, sun, moon and stars and get married to them all. So I marry everything in the creation. My whole life is a continuous marriage. Yoga means this mystical marriage. There is a marriage within myself. There is a marriage between man and man, between man and woman, between man and nature, between man and God.

Man's experience of his relation with God and the world is expressed and explained most effectively through the symbolism of marriage. A marriage is between two personalities, the feminine and the masculine. When we consider God in relation to man, God is male and man is female. There is marriage between God and man. Yahweh is male and Israel is female. There is marriage between Yahweh and Israel.

The world is female, and there is marriage between God and the world. Heaven is male and earth is female. There is marriage between heaven and earth. Look at the trees. There are male and female trees. So there is marriage between the trees. For example the peepul tree and the neem tree. The two trees are planted together and grow together as one. The tree is seen as a symbol of marriage. The marriage between heaven and earth takes place in the tree. Yogis, Rishis and Munis sit under a tree and meditate. It is said that when a devotee came and saw Buddha under the holy tree, she mistook the man for a manifestation of a tree spirit. The enlightenment of the Muni is considered as a marriage. A Muni sits under a tree and meditates. In primitive religion the spirit of the ancestors and the supernatural powers are identified together as one. And it is believed that this supernatural power, what we call the Spirit of God, is present in the tree. The tree spirit and this Spirit enter into the Muni who sits in meditation under the tree and awakens the spirit of the Muni and the marriage of the Muni takes place. The enlightenment of the Muni is the marriage of the Muni with the tree. That is why the Muni is identified with the holy tree. The union between God and man takes place through the tree. The birth of the enlightened man results from the marital union of the Spirit of God and the spirit of man. An enlightened Muni is born from the holy tree and he is the living presence of God on earth.

This is seen in primitive religion. If a village girl is unable to have a child, she prays before a sacred tree to the forces of fertility, and she will hang a toy-cradle from its branches or even in certain cases she will get impregnated by the Muni who sits under the tree, if he wills to act on behalf of the spirit. In some villages a girl is first married to a tree. Only in this way will she be fruitful in her marriage to man. This is because the spirits which are to enter into the womb of women are first in trees. It is believed that the tree spirit comes from the ancestors, from the moon, from God. A girl who is going to marry a man first gets married to a tree. Here the tree is male. The tree stands for the spirit of the ancestors, the Spirit of God, and this spirit too is male. So, when a girl gets married to a tree, it means that she gets married to God prior to her marriage with man. This marriage is the mystical marriage. And it reveals that the woman conceives a child not just by the marital act but also from God's Spirit. Of course the Spirit of God works through the marital union of a man and a woman.

Jesus Christ the son of man, the Son of God, is born from the blessed virgin Mary who conceived by the Holy Spirit. The Spirit of God entered into the womb of Mary and she conceived a child. Jesus is born to reveal the mystical marriage, mystical union, mystical birth. The church is married to Jesus Christ. We are married to Jesus and to God. The whole humanity shares the inner life of God through the mystical marriage with God in Jesus Christ by the Holy Spirit.

In God Himself we may speak of a male and a female aspect.[1] There is an ancient Christian tradition[2] according to which the Father represents the male aspect of God and the Holy Spirit the female aspect. "The Hebrew tradition was patriarchal and Christianity has preserved only a masculine concept of God. The Father and the Son are masculine in their very names, and even the Spirit, which is neuter in Greek, has been given a masculine character. But the Hebrew tradition also preserves a word for the spirit (*ruah*) which is feminine, and in the Syrian Church this feminine gender was preserved, so that they could speak of the Holy Spirit as Mother. There is also in the Old Testament the beautiful figure of Wisdom (*hokhmah*) which is also feminine. In this we can find a truly feminine aspect of God when it is said: 'She is a breath of the power of God and a pure emanation of the glory of the almighty, and again: she is a reflection of eternal light and a spotless mirror of the working of God . . . though she is but

[1]Prov. 8:22-31: Sirach 24:3-12; Wisdom 7:22-30; Isaiah 49:15.
[2]Journal of Dharma Vol. V, No. 2, pp. 162-164.

one, she can do all things, and remaining in herself, she renews all things' — *Wisdom* 7: 25-27.[3] "

According to the Oriental Christian tradition the power of the Father which is the Spirit *(ruah)* is feminine. This is in some way similar to the Hindu religious experience in which the power of *Sakti* of Shiva is feminine. Religions see distinctions and union within Godhead. It shows an inner dynamics in God which is reflected on earth, especially in marital relationship. Marital relationship is obviously a deep relationship between two persons. In human marriage the distinction between two persons is overcome by the bond of love and marital commitment. This reminds us of that eternal marriage taking place in God where the inner distinctions of persons in God are constantly overcome in an abiding union. Thus it could be said that human marriage on earth reflects the divine marriage. God created man in his image and likeness. What is in God is reflected in man. Not only by marriage does man participate in this inner dynamics of God. Every man is called to enter into the divine mystical marriage within himself, with the whole humanity, with the whole creation and with God.

A Yogi in order to grow in mystical marital union sits in meditation and breathes in man and woman, animals, birds, plants, mountains, valleys, rivers, sun and moon and stars and everything in the creation and breathes himself out to them in and through Yeshu and Abba.

[3]Bede Griffiths: The Marriage of East and West, London (Collins) 1982, p. 191.

6. *Attachment to the Parents, Relatives and Friends*

I was so much loved by my parents and I loved them so much. My departure from home to join the Ashram caused a tremendous pain of separation felt by my parents and in me. In order to overcome the absence of my parents I was told not to think of them all the time. I must detach myself from my parents in order to follow Christ. I took literally the scriptural saying "If any one wants to follow me let him renounce everything, hate your father and mother and follow me" (Mt 8:34). So I took a kind of negative attitude toward my parents. I tried to think of them only when I prayed for them or when I got a letter from them or when I wrote to them. Other times I kept them out of my mind. Especially in meditation when I concentrated on Jesus the thoughts of my parents came in and disturbed me. But I tried to forget them and to concentrate on Jesus. Gradually, without knowing, I started suppressing the deep-rooted desire of having the presence of my parents. Through the suppression of the feelings and desires to a certain extent I succeeded in concentration in meditation. But after two years, one day suddenly all the suppressed feelings and desires started coming back and a strong feeling of the absence of my father and mother and I was so seized by an uncontrollable desire to see my mother and father that I wanted to go home.

I began the Yogic meditation. I started breathing in my mother with all my heart, soul and strength in and through Yeshu. I breathed myself out to her in and through Abba. Here my mother is the figure of Jesus. Of course it was very easy for me to concentrate on her because I love her and I am attached to her. While I breathe in, Jesus enters within as my mother and takes me into his body consciousness so that I and my mother are one in his body and he takes us to his Father. I continued this meditation for some days and gradually I began to experience that my mother was close to me, closer than myself is close to me. I began to feel her presence in me more and more. Some times I experienced that I was in the womb of my mother. And I was so happy to be there, in a most secure and comfortable home. I experienced God as my mother and myself in her womb. This experience controlled my desire to see her and the feeling that she was very far from me. It doesn't mean that after this meditation I had no more desire to go home and see her. It only means I am not just living merely in the physical body consciousness. Of course I have to continuously go on meditating in order to grow more and more in Yeshu-Abba Consciousness, in Cosmic Christ Body Consciousness.

Then what does the saying that to follow Jesus one has to hate his father, mother and relatives really mean? In order to give birth to the Cosmic Christ Body Consciousness, the individual body consciousness has to die. That means I must die in order to give birth to my mother. If I do not die, I will not be able to see my mother, I will see only myself. By this death I am not disappearing but I am finding myself in my mother's womb. I enter into the state of consciousness where I experience myself and my mother as one body. To hate your father and mother means breaking oneself from the attachments of the individual body consciousness, which enables one to enter into Yeshu-Abba Consciousness. One has to die to this state of attachment in order to follow Jesus or to give birth to Jesus. Through this detachment I discover Jesus and in Jesus I find my parents and relatives. In order to see my parents in Jesus, I have to undergo the experience of death, or breaking through, from the lower state of consciousness where I see only myself and my parents.

Renouncing and hating father and mother, relatives and friends, literally, in order to follow Jesus, is against Yogic teaching. Yoga teaches Ahimsa — non-violence, non-hatred. And also it is against the Ten Commandments. "Love your father and mother, love your neighbour as yourself." To-day no psychologist would tell you to hate your father and mother. Cultivate positive detachment and a positive attitude towards everything.

Attachment to relatives and friends becomes an obstacle for meditation. Follow the same technique breathing in your friend and breathing yourself out to him in and through Yeshu and Abḇa.

PART IV

FAMILY MEDITATION — MARRIED COUPLE

PART IV

FAMILY MEDITATION — MARRIED COUPLE

Let a husband and wife sit face to face in meditation. Begin the meditation with eyes opened. Look at each other. Become aware of the presence of Jesus our Lord and Master. The husband sees Jesus in his wife and his wife sees Jesus in her husband. Husband and wife sing the mantra. 'Om Nama Christaya' with all their hearts, minds and strength, vocally, then mentally and then they sit in silence. Then in the second stage of meditation they must become aware of the breathing where the breath comes from and where it goes. The husband breathes in the wife in and through Yeshu and breathes himself out to her. The wife breathes in to the husband in and through Yeshu and breathes herself out to him. For the husband the wife is the visible presence of Jesus. Jesus is coming to him as his wife with all her good and bad qualities, as she really is, with all her feelings and affection, love and concern. The husband with open heart must welcome his wife the way she comes to him. The husband if he has any misunderstanding or guilt feeling or anger, he must become aware of that and without hiding or suppressing them, he must offer them with Jesus to his wife. For the wife the husband is the visible presence of Jesus. Jesus is coming to her as her husband with all his good and bad qualities, as he really is, with all his feelings and affection, love and concern. The wife with open heart must welcome her husband the way he comes to her. If the wife has any misunderstanding or guilt feeling or anger, she must become aware of them and without hiding or suppressing them, must give them to her husband with Jesus. Thus both husband and wife in Jesus undergo the purification and become the body of Christ.

While breathing in mentally repeat the mantra Yē and while breathing out Ā. In and through Yeshu and Abba, breathe in and breathe out. Begin the breathing in and breathing out with eyes opened and then gradually close the eyes. Be fully present, aware of what is really happening. Go deeper and deeper into the movement between the husband and wife. In and through Yeshu and Abba the husband moves towards his wife and the wife moves towards her husband. The husband enters into his wife and the wife enters into her husband in and through Jesus and both undergo the purification of the experience of death in Jesus. Finally they become one body, the Mystical Body of Christ. Here the spirit of the husband and the spirit of the wife meet together in the Spirit of Jesus. The will and the mind of the husband and the mind and the will of the wife enter into the mind and the will of Jesus. The husband dies in order to give birth to his wife in him and the wife dies in order to give birth to her husband in her. The husband and wife die in Christ in order to take new birth in Christ. Both husband and wife find themselves in Christ — as the Mystical Body of Christ.

After the meditation the husband and wife come out as new persons with new awareness and new visions. They come out with one body consciousness, Cosmic Christ Body Consciousness, Yeshu Abba Consciousness. They will live together as one body. The husband will be able to understand the wife and the wife will be able to understand the husband because the mind of the husband and the mind of the wife work through the mind of Christ. The meditation will help the husband and wife to build up a beautiful marital life. Very often what happens in married life is that the husband and wife are not able to understand each other. The husband will act according to his will and the wife will act according to her will. Both will start shouting at each other. Anger, hatred, lack of affection and love, misunderstanding, etc., enter into their life. Thus the marital life becomes a chaos. It is because the husband lives and acts on one level of consciousness and the wife lives and acts on another level of consciousness. Unless both enter into the same level of consciousness, they will not be able to understand each other. Or we can put it in this way: the husband and wife are both living and acting just in the individual body consciousness which is conditioned by time, matter, space, senses, emotions, feelings, desires, thought, etc. On this level of consciousness, one acts more from self-interest and for self-satisfaction. The ego will be predominant in this consciousness. Because of the short sightedness of the ego one will not be able to see the needs and interest of the other. Remaining on this level of consciousness, just going on shouting at each other will not help them in any way to understand each other. Both persons must die and enter into a common consciousness, what we call 'we' consciousness, community consciousness, Cosmic Consciousness, Christ Consciousness or Mystical Body Consciousness. Then they will be able to understand each other, then they will be able to live together in love, joy and peace.

Husband! Breathe in your wife in and through Jesus. Wife! Breathe in your husband in and through Jesus. Husband! Breathe yourself out to the wife in and through Abba. Wife! Breathe yourself out to the husband in and through Abba.

If you have children keep them also with you in meditation. Sit as a circle so that everyone in the circle can see each other. Then continue the same meditation. The husband will breathe in the wife and the children and the wife will breathe in the husband and the children in and through Yeshu. The children will breathe in the father and the mother in and through Yeshu. Follow the same pattern while breathing out Abba. Gradually all will grow in family consciousness, father, mother and children as one body. Through Yeshu - Abba Consciousness they will be able to enter into the Trinitarian Family and experience the love, joy and peace of this family. Through this family consciousness the children will be able to understand the parents and the parents will be able to understand the children; they will grow as a beautiful family of Father, Son and Holy Spirit.

PART V

COMMUNITY MEDITATION — HOW TO GROW IN COMMUNITY CONSCIOUSNESS

1 Introduction.

2 What is Meant by Community Consciousness.

3 Technique of Community Meditation

PART V

COMMUNITY MEDITATION — HOW TO GROW IN COMMUNITY CONSCIOUSNESS

1. *Introduction*

There are different types of communities: priests, seminarians, brothers, sisters, lay women and lay men. This form of meditation can be used in any of these communities in order to grow in community consciousness. In any community there will be a leader or coordinator to keep the community in harmony and also for its proper functioning. The question is how to grow in community consciousness in order to build up a better community.

2. *What is Meant by Community Consciousness*

If I want to live in community, and the community wants to grow together to its fullness, each member of the community must enter into community consciousness. Example: two persons are living together. If they want to live in love, joy and peace they must know each other. Suppose both of them are limited by their own individual consciousness, they cannot live together. Because I have my own consciousness and he has his own consciousness my activity will be limited within his consciousness. What I say, he cannnot agree with because he cannot understand it, and in the same way when he speaks, if I want to understand him I must know him, that means I must enter into his consciousness. When my consciousness is in his consciousness, I understand and accept what he says. In the same way his consciousness must enter into my consciousness and he must adjust his consciousness according to my consciousness. Then he will be able to understand me and accept what I say. Now both of us together form a common consciousness which we call community consciousness. Now where is our individual consciousness? Our individual consciousness has died. This death should be understood in its mystical sense. Through the death of the individual consciousness the community consciousness has to undergo the experience of death or the pain of death. Now I am no more just conditioned by 'I' and 'you' consciousness, but I am in 'we' consciousness. Then where is I and you? Though it underwent death, it is there in 'WE', but on a different level of consciousness.

Now there is a problem which arises with entering into community consciousness. If we are two in the community it will not be so difficult. I can without much difficulty open to him and he can open to me. There are different ways in which one can open to the other. For example, through dialogue and sharing; giving my own life history and what I think and wish about myself, and what I think about him and what I wish him to be. And he must give his life history to me and what he thinks and wishes me to be. Then both come to a common understanding while both have to admit their own weakness and limitations. Then both will have to undergo the pain of death and the experience of death. This ideal may be applied to the bigger community also.

But the community which is a bigger one may not find it so easy to open itself like this. Still we must try our best. In the big community we must approach the leader of the community. A true leader will have community consciousness. Each of the members approach the leader and through the consciousness of the leader each comes to the consciousness of each member. When all the members come to the consciousness of the leader, then the community takes birth. When all the members have community consciousness, the community will be able to fulfil the aim for which the community is formed. The leader of the community has a plan and purpose about its members.

The whole of mankind is one community and the Son of Man or Cosmic Man is the head. St. Paul says Christ is the head and the whole creation is His body. "Things on earth and things in heaven gathered together in unity in Christ." Christ had this community consciousness when He said "I am the vine and you are the branches" and "Father, may all be one in us as you are in me and I am in You." We are all the members of the Mystical Body of Christ. We are all called to enter into the Cosmic Christ Body Consciousness and experience that we all belong to one family, one community as the children of God the Father.

3. *Technique of Community Meditation*

Sit together in a circle in meditation posture. Begin the meditation with eyes open. Look at each other. Become aware of the saying of Jesus, "where two or three are gathered together I will be in the midst of them." It is the Spirit of our Master, Lord Jesus Christ which brought us together and his Spirit will open our hearts and minds and enable us to recognise our Master, and sing his Name. Start singing the Name, 'Om Nama Christaya' vocally, then mentally and then in silence with all your heart and mind and strength. Come to the awareness of breathing where the breath comes from and where it goes. Breathe in every member of the community one after the other in and through Yeshu and breathe oneself out in and through Abba to everyone, one after the other. While breathing in receive the other as he or she is. While breathing out give yourself as you are. Take in the other person with the breath to the depth of your being and give yourself to the other with the breath from the depth of your being. You must feel this movement of receiving and giving while breathing in and breathing out. Be fully aware of yourself during the meditation. Many things will happen. Things which we never dreamed of will happen. The effects of past actions which have gone down to the subconscious will be awakened to the conscious mind. Let your mind be alert to face the consequences. There will be a mutual self-giving and sharing in deep silence if everyone in the group is open to the working of the Spirit. If for example one is not open but closes himself, then the community will sense it. For example, if one member in the group is having anger towards another member and if that anger is awakened, surely the whole group will get the vibration. The group will feel that there is some bad force. The ones who are deeper in meditation will receive the vibration faster. The moment one receives this evil vibration, he welcomes it and absorbs into his body with that particular person, if that person is clear to him, and undergoes the purification with Jesus by his power and transforms that evil force or re-creates the good force and sends it through his breath to that particular person and to the whole community in and through Abba. The more the community enters into the Mysical Body consciousness or Yeshu-Abba Consciousness, the more the community can feel what is happening within the community. Gradually the community grows into the experience of love, joy and peace in Yeshu-Abba Consciousness. In order to come to this experience each individual has to empty himself and give birth to the community or the Mystical Body of Christ.

Do not come to the conclusion that in community meditation one has to go on thinking about the other and breathing in the other all through the meditation. If you have the one hour for meditation, do breathing in the other consciously for fifteen minutes or half an hour and then the rest of the time enter into deep silence with the awareness of the movement from Father to Son and Son to the Father, God to man and man to God, receiving and giving. In this state one allows himself to be moved by the movement of the Spirit and to experience the Trinitarian life of God. In this state one experiences the ultimate reality beyond the senses, thoughts, words and actions. But to come to this level one has to go through the various levels of consciousness and purification. To experience the ultimate reality in the stillness of the mind and body, one has to master to a certain extent at least the harmony of these three levels of consciousness (1) individual consciousness, or I consciousness or dual consciousness (2) community consciousness or Cosmic Consciousness or Cosmic Christ Consciousness. (3) superconsciousness or God Consciousness or Father Consciousness.

During the community meditation the Spirit of Jesus and the Father awakens the spirit of each individual. The whole community is awakened to the working of the Spirit. Each one must be opened to the Spirit and listen to the voice of the Spirit. When the spirit of the individuals meets in the Spirit of Jesus and the Father, lots of sharing communication will take place. We can really feel the working of the Holy Spirit in a very marvellous way. In this state of consciousness the Yogic charismatic prayer begins where the Spirit takes full possession of us. The Spirit moves each one to the other. The Spirit moves the whole group. The Holy Spirit awakens the various forces of good and bad in us and disturbs us in order to purify us. In this state each one will manifest his own or her own real nature, i.e., good and bad temperament. Fear and anxiety may come, joy and peace may come. Anything may happen. It only means that what we are really will be manifested. What is hidden will come to the light. We must express either in silence or in action. The Yogi believes in silence and communication to God, world and men in the stillness of the mind, body and senses. But the Yogi will not suppress the needs of the mind, body and senses to express and communicate in action, thoughts and words. He allows them to come up and slowly leads them to silence and transforms them to the subtle vibrations. He senses these vibrations through prana, through spirit. Thus the communication takes place in deep silence through the subtle vibrations of the spirit. This form of communication is most powerful, effective and life-giving. The vibration, the message, love, joy, peace, power, grace, life goes out from the whole body of the Yogi, from the whole body of Yogic community which is the Mystical Body of the Cosmic Man, Jesus Christ. Conclude the meditation with sending the love, joy and peace vibrations. In and through Yeshu-Abba Consciousness, breathe out through your whole body the love, joy and peace to each one in the community and breathe in through your whole body the love, joy and peace from each one. End the Yogic meditation with chanting 'Om Shanti' three times.

PART VI

YOGA NIDRA MEDITATION AND SUBCONSCIOUS HEALING

PART VI

YOGA NIDRA MEDITATION
AND
SUBCONSCIOUS HEALING

Introduction

The purpose of Yoga Nidra is to give conscious rest to the physical, mental and psychic body. These exercises increase the power of self-awareness of the physical body, mental body and psychic body and eventually to the spiritual body. The highest form of Yogic meditation is the conscious rest of the physical, mental, psychic and spiritual body. Today the world is full of tension and unrest. In some way or other every person is in unrest. The science of Yoga teaches us the ways and means to give maximum rest to the different levels of body-consciousness. This exercise improves the power of self-awareness. Very often we do not know what is happening in our body and what is the cause for various symptoms taking place in the body. For example one often gets a headache or a stomach pain, cough, cold, dryness of the throat and lips, extreme cold or heat in the body, now and then pain in certain parts of the body. These various kinds of symptoms are taking place in our body and very often we feel them only when it becomes very intense or severe. Why is one not able to feel the sensations or symptoms when it is more subtle? It is because one's self-awareness is not well developed. By practice of Yoga Nidra one becomes more and more sensitive to the gross and subtle sensations of the body. At every moment in all our body there are various kinds of sensations, pleasant and unpleasant. Through self-awareness one will be able to discover the cause and effect of anything that happens in the body, the cause of various kinds of tension and of illness physical, mental and psychological. Once we know the cause and effect, then we will be able to control them or heal them or channel them in the right direction. If we know the root cause of a particular tension in its subtle state we can prevent its further growth. Once we are sure of the cause and bad effects of various tensions on our physical, mental and psychic body, then we will not generate such tensions. Tensions are generated through various actions and events in our life, whether good or bad.

When our senses are active, when our mind and intellect are active, we generate more and more samskaras, i.e. effect of our actions. Any action will have an effect on us and some symptoms will manifest in our body immediately. Also any action will have an effect on our sub-conscious and the symptoms will manifest in our physical body. An example will make it clear. Some people have a terrible fear of certain animals, creatures, fear of particular people, fear of darkness, fear to be alone, fear of silence, fear of the graveyard, fear of woman, fear of man, fear of old people, fear of sound, fear of a crowd, etc. There are various kinds of causes for this fear. We have no need to go into all these in detail. From the moment we were born, or even when we were in our mother's womb, and all through our childhood, teenage, till now innumerable events took place which caused fear in us. The effect of the fear has gone in to our sub-conscious from the time we were in our mother's womb onwards. By nature itself this fear is released all through our life. Certain types of outside objects, persons, sounds or events can awaken this fear from one's sub-conscious and the symptoms will manifest in one's physical body; sometimes as violent reactions, like anger; sometimes the person will cry, sometimes he will laugh loudly; sometimes the whole body gets cold; sometimes the person will collapse. The symptoms can be in any form. Or a certain type of person may get attached to and respond to a person of another type. Sometimes this type of person will develop certain types of bad character. In extreme cases when these fears are suddenly awakened from the sub-conscious, a nervous breakdown will take place. There is always a tendency in a person to avoid outside objects and situations which awaken the fear within and it leads to the suppression of the feelings.

Yogic meditation and Yoga Nidra are the means to awaken various kinds of tensions which are suppressed and hidden in the subconscious. What happens is that when one stops the external activities of the senses and the mind and gets into the stillness of the body, the senses and the mind, then what is in our sub-conscious will come to the conscious mind and the symptoms will arise in our nervous system and the body. That means that when we stop generating various symptoms through the external activities of the senses and the mind, then what is already generated from our childhood and has gone into the sub-conscious mind, will manifest as symptoms in the body. It is something like where we stop eating, the body starts using what is in our body till everything is used up. Once all that is buried in the sub-conscious has been brought up, then freedom, liberation, emptiness, Moksha will be attained. Just imagine a person who is free from physical, mental and psychological tensions. *Such a person will experience love, joy and peace of the spiritual body.* He will be able to live, act and behave with full freedom of the conscious mind. He will be able to discern the good and evil and choose what is good for his physical, mental, psychic and spiritual growth and well-being. Such a person will be able to know where he came from, why he is living in this world and where he is going. He knows the purpose of his existence. He will have the vision of reality. For him there is meaning in life. He will not blame God by asking: "Why have you created me?" He will not curse himself and God for being in this body. Rather it will be a great joy for him to have this body and the world around. These types of people Jesus meant when he said "Blessed are the pure in heart for they shall see God" (Mt. 5:8) "Blessed are you poor; for yours is the kingdom of God" (Lk. 6:20). The one who is pure in thoughts, words and action, [physically, mentally, psychologically and spiritually] and the one who is poor, that means without any tension, the liberated person [physically, mentally, psychologically and spiritually] will experience God and his kingdom. Buddha teaches the attainment of Nirvana through the experience of the emptiness of the physical, mental, psychological and spiritual bodies. A Yogi enters into Samadhi or Kaivalya through this liberation from the various tensions of the physical, mental, psychic and spiritual bodies. All the religious teachers teach the liberation of man, the freedom of man from physical, mental, psychic and spiritual bondage.

Jesus identifies his teaching with that of the prophets by reading the utterance of the prophet Isaiah "The Spirit of the Lord is upon me .... He has sent me to proclaim release to the captives, recovering sight to the blind, to set at liberty those who are oppressed"(Lk. 4:18). Yoga Nidra is a scientific teaching which is applicable to any man in any religion, cast or creed. This exercise will help him to fulfill the higher values of his life.

TECHNIQUE OF YOGA NIDRA

1. *First Day*

Sit in Stira Sukhasana steady and pleasant posture for meditation. Once you sit in one posture there should not be any movement of any part of the body. The total stillness of the body is required to get maximum benefit of this exercise. One must be able to sit for at least half an hour. One hour would be better. This exercise can be done for half an hour, one hour, two hours or more at a stretch or with intervals.

Keep the body and the mind still and relaxed, and the eyes closed. Become aware of the top of the head, the centre and then all around the centre of the head. Just be aware of that particular area at that time; be aware of what is happening there; be aware of the various sensations which arise and vanish, the gross sensations and subtle sensations. Do not make any judgement. There will be pleasant and unpleasant sensations. Do not get attached to any sensation. Just be aware, realize what is happening. With awareness you will realize that sensations are arising and vanishing. It is not permanent but changing. One should not get lost or get attached in these changing sensations, pleasant or unpleasant.

Slowly pass the awareness from the top of the head to the forehead, both sides of the head, back of the head, eyebrows, eyes, nose, lips, left cheek, right cheek, chin, left ear, right ear, front of the neck, both sides, back. Do not spend too long in one particular area. A few seconds will do. See that there is no movement in any part of your body.

Come to the left shoulder, down to the elbow, elbow to the wrist, each finger and thumb, palm, the front of the upper chest both sides, under the armpit, back, mid-chest, both sides, back, abdomen, front, the navel, both sides of the abdomen, around the waist, genital organ, left thigh, from thigh to knee, knee to the ankle, heel, sole of the foot, toes. Come to the right thigh, from thigh to the knee, knee to the ankle, heel, sole of the foot and toes.

Now start from toes to the head. Left foot, toes, sole of the foot, heel, ankle, ankle to the knee, knee to thigh, genital organ, waist, right foot, toes, sole of the foot, heel, ankle, ankle to the knee, knee to thigh, thigh to the waist, around the waist, front of the abdomen, navel, both sides of the abdomen, back, mid-chest, front, both sides, back, upper chest, front, both sides, back, front of the neck, both sides and back, chin, lips, nose, eyes, eyebrows, cheek, both sides, ears, forehead, back of the head and finally to the top of the head. Continue this exercise from the top of the head to the toes from the toes to the top of the head. Once or twice more. At the end for five minutes at least remain without doing anything, just watching what is happening, just be aware of the whole body. Just experience silence, peace, stillness of the body. Then lie down flat on the ground for five or ten minutes, just experiencing the silence of the body and mind.

2. *Second Day*

On the second day repeat the same exercise from top of the head to the toes and then toes to the head two rounds. And then remain seated and continue the following new exercise. Turn your mind inside your body, that means look inside. Become aware of what is happening inside your body, and feel the various sensations, gross and subtle sensations.

Become aware inside the top of the head, the brain, just be aware of the various sensations, slowly come down to the tongue, teeth, palate, inside both ears, the throat, heart, lungs, stomach, small and big intestine, inside the navel, the kidneys, inner parts of the genital organ, go through the muscles, nerves and bones to the knee, knee to heel, sole of the foot and toes of the left leg and then to the right leg through the thigh, knee, heel, sole of the foot to the toes.

Now start from the toes to the head, the right foot inside the right toes and go through the sole of the foot, heel, ankle, ankle to the knee, knee to the thigh, waist, left foot, toes, sole of the foot, heel, ankle, ankle to the knee, knee to the thigh, waist. Inside the genital organ, stomach, small and big intestines, heart, lungs, throat, tongue, teeth, the palate, upper palate, inside the ears, brain and finally to the top of the head. Also the spine, from top of the spine to the base of the spine and from the base of the spine to the top of the spine. While going through the body be aware of the bones, nerves and muscles. Repeat this exercise two rounds.

Then for five minutes just sit without doing anything, just be aware of what is happening in your body and mind. Experience the silence, the peace and stillness of the body and mind.

And then the last five or ten minutes lie down flat on the ground and remain in stillness with the awareness and experience of what is happening in your body, the silence and peace. Remember the last ten or fifteen minutes are most important when you are not doing anything but with the awareness experiencing what is happening in your body inside and outside.

3. *Third Day*

Repeat the first day exercise and the second day exercise from the top of the head to the toes and from the toes to the top of the head outside and inside the body. Then lie down flat on the ground and do the Savasana, relaxation exercise. Remember when you lie down flat on the ground to keep the feet wide apart, open the heels, both hands on both sides a little away from the body, palms open, the back of the head flat on the ground as if a pillow was beneath the head while the chin comes closer to the upper chest and eyes closed. Keep the whole body and the neck straight.

Now you are going to give conscious relaxation to all parts of the body. The secret of the relaxation depends very much on the attitude of your mind. It is you yourself who are going to give rest to each part of your body consciously. Try to be fully present in your body. Once you have got the posture, see that there is no movement in any part of your body. Give mental suggestion to your whole body to let your body gravitate towards the earth. You are going to experience the death of your body, a total detachment from your individual body consciousness. Just be aware of what is happening to your body and mind. Be fully present in your body.

Imagine that you are sinking down into the ground. Once again imagine that you are sinking down into the ground. Allow yourself to be relaxed, to be released from all the tension, anxieties and worries. You are made out of earth. Feel that you are one with the earth.

Become aware of your left foot, toes, sole of the foot, heel, ankle, ankle to the knee, knee to thigh, waist. Up to the waist left leg relaxed. Forget your left leg. Detach yourself from your left leg. Let it go down and merge into the ground and become part of the earth. Become aware of the right foot, toes, sole of the foot, heel, ankle, ankle to knee, knee to thigh, waist. Now both legs relaxed. Imagine that you are sinking down into the ground. Become aware of the genital organ, abdomen, front, both sides, back, mid-chest front, both sides, back, upper chest, front, both sides, back. Up to the neck the whole body relaxed. Come to the left hand, fingers, palm, wrist, wrist to the elbow, elbow to the shoulder. Right hand fingers, palm, wrist, wrist to the elbow, elbow to the shoulder. Become aware of the neck, front, both sides, back, chin, lips, nose, eyes, eyebrows, cheek, ears, back of the head, forehead and top of the head. Now the whole body is relaxed. Imagine once again that you are sinking down into the ground, towards the earth. Earth has its power to absorb all the impurities, tensions from your body. You just allow yourself to undergo the purification.

Now start the exercise from the top of the head to the toes.

Become aware of the top of the head, forehead, back of the head, ears, cheeks, eyebrows, eyes, nose, mouth, lips, chin, front of the neck, both sides, back. Left shoulder, up to the elbow, elbow to the wrist, palm, fingers, thumb. Right shoulder, up to the elbow, elbow to the wrist, palm, fingers, thumb. Become aware of the front of the upper chest, both sides, back, mid-chest, front, both sides, back. Abdomen, front, both sides, back, around the waist, genital organ, left thigh, thigh to the knee, knee to the ankle, heel, sole of the foot, toes. Right thigh, thigh to the knee, knee to the ankle, heel, sole of the foot, toes. Imagine once again that you are sinking down into the ground. Now you are one with the earth, the whole body is relaxed. There is no movement in any part of the body. Now the breathing is very slow. Just be there watching your breath where the breath comes from and where it goes. Just like a third person. If any thought comes, let it come and go. You just watch your breathing. Let your mind flow with the movement of the breath and undergo the experience of death, total detachment from your individual body consciousness. Earth is your body, you are one with the earth. Remain in this state five to ten minutes.

You gave conscious relaxation to each part of your body. You underwent the experience of death. Now you are going to give life to your body. You are going to come out as new man with new awareness. Become aware of your abdomen and of the abdominal breathing. Take in as much air as you can and then breathe out all the air. Repeat six times. Now you are going to give conscious life to each part of your body. Become aware of your left foot. Move little by little your toes, the right foot, move the toes, move your right fingers, left fingers. Slowly move your head both sides, move both legs, hands, head. Breathe deeply in and out with upper chest. Become aware of your whole body, the atmosphere around you, the world around you. Open your eyes and close slowly, come out of the relaxation with new awareness as new man. Turn your whole body to the right. Lie down on your right side with right elbow bent beneath your hand as a pillow. After one or two minutes slowly come up sideways with the support of the left palm placed on the ground in front. Sit in your meditation posture with the eyes closed. Experience what is happening in your body and mind. Just remain without doing anything but experience the silence, the peace, the rest at least five minutes.

4. *Fourth Day*

Repeat the first day exercise, second day exercise and third day exercise. That means sit in meditation posture and become aware of the top of the head to the toes and toes to the head. First outside the body and then inside. Then lie down on your back and do the Savasana — relaxation exercise from the toes to the head and head to the toes. Remain in the lying down posture and continue the following exercise.

Now turn your mind inside your body. You are going to give conscious rest to the inner parts of the body. Become aware of the left foot. Get inside the toes and go through the whole body inside, giving conscious rest to each part one after the other, the nerves, muscles, bones, etc., and finally reach to the top of the head. Then start from the top of the head to the toes. That means on the second day you did this exercise sitting. Now do the same exercise in lying down posture.

At the end go through your whole body inside and outside and see if there is any part of your body which is not relaxed. If there is any tension or something wrong in any part of your body in this state while all the rest of your body is relaxed, you will be able to locate it immediately. If there is, then become aware of that particular area of the body and send the prana, the life force, the breath, and then allow that part to relax, to undergo the purification.

Now the whole body is relaxing. Imagine that you are sinking down to the ground. You are going to experience the death of your body one with Jesus Christ, the Cosmic Man in the tomb. Earth is the tomb and you are in the tomb with Jesus undergoing the purification. Allow yourself to be burnt in the fire of the earth, the fire of the tomb, the fire of the womb of the Mother Earth, the fire of the Shakti, the feminine power. Allow oneself to be burnt, to be transformed, to be born again by the spirit of the Mother Earth, the Cosmic Mother. You have entered into the womb of the Cosmic Mother Earth with Jesus Christ the Cosmic Man in order to be transformed and born again with the Cosmic Body Consciousness.

Just be there in the womb of the Cosmic Mother watching the movement of the breath, the Cosmic Spirit. Allow yourself to be moved by the movement of the Cosmic Spirit. Let your mind flow into the breath and be there, allowing yourself to undergo the experience of death, the total detachment from your individual body consciousness. Let the Mother Earth, the Cosmic Mother, the Holy Spirit, give you a new birth in the Cosmic Man, Jesus Christ. Remain in this state ten minutes or more. Yoga Nidra is a conscious sleep in the womb of the Cosmic Mother Earth. God is experienced as a Cosmic

Mother Earth, Yoga Nidra means sleep consciously in the womb of God.

After ten minutes slowly come out of Yoga Nidra with the new awareness as a new man and sit in meditation posture for five minutes or more experiencing the new life. When you open your eyes, you will have a new vision, you will see everything in a new way in the light of the Risen Lord. You died with Jesus and you have risen with Jesus and you live with Jesus.

PART VII

KUNDALINI SHAKTI YOGA — THE SERPENT POWER

PART VII

KUNDALINI SHAKTI YOGA — THE SERPENT POWER

Introduction

One day I saw a serpent (Cobra) dancing in the evening sunlight. I just looked at the serpent with all my attention and I experienced Jesus, dancing as a serpent. Prior to this experience one night in a wakeful state, I had a vision of Jesus sitting in bright light. The face of Jesus was radiating love, joy and peace in its fulness. It took several months and years for me to understand what this experience was. After this experience I became more and more interested in the serpent. I started meditating to discover the hidden mystery of the serpent. I began to wonder what was happening to me. Before, I used to hate the serpent because I was taught that the serpent is the symbol of the devil, but now the serpent had become the symbol of Jesus. There came to my mind the quotation from the Bible: "As Moses lifted up the serpent in the wilderness, so must the Son of Man be lifted up, that whoever believes in him may have eternal life" (Jn. 3:14). This experience led me to Kundalini Shakti Yoga.

Yogic experience of the mysterious supernatural power and the natural power identified together hidden at the base of the spine is expressed as 'Kundalini Shakti,' the Serpent Power. It is experienced that this serpent is lying coiled at the base of the spine of man, sleeping in the unconscious or fathomless consciousness of man, coiled around the navel of the cosmos, lying in the depths of the ocean. This mysterious force of the unconscious coiled at the base of the spine is identified with the emotive forces of the libido. The purpose of Yoga is to lift this Serpent Power, drawing it up, into the spinal column, through the six chakras, each of which is a nerve centre of the body. The path of the Kundalini seems to reach from one spiral to another, for each center of the body, is itself seen as a spiral. The libido then travels upwards from the navel, seat of all man's instinctual urges, to the crown of his head where the life force is transmuted into the pure fire of the mind. In fact the journey of the serpent upwards, is marked by fire, because intense heat is felt in the body as Kundalini rises. Reversely the journey of the serpent downwards is indicated by chilling coldness. This rising of Kundalini means enlightenment. This light radiates the whole body and mind and the whole world around as life-giving light.

1. *Evolution of Man's Experience of the Supernatural Power from Cosmic Serpent to Cosmic Man Siva*

Siva is the father of all the enlightened ones, the Yogis, and he is ever in Cosmic Consciousness. He is the Cosmic Man, the source of poison and amrita (Ambrosia), the destruction and recreation; and this is represented by the serpent, hanging around his neck like a garland with his hair streaming out in the cosmic dance like serpents. Where the forces of the unconscious are brought to the conscious level, the harmony and integrity of the person is achieved. This is what the story of the churning of the milky ocean means.

The mythology goes thus: The cosmic ocean or Milky ocean was churned by the antipodal forces of Devas and Asuras. While churning the ocean, the first substance, which comes to the surface prior to eternal life, the Amrita, is poison. It is the poison of the serpent, which is the natural concomitant of the elixir of life, that comes as the first fruit of the churning of the cosmic ocean. This poison is not possible for man, gods or demons to assimilate, because it is the cosmic force of destruction. Only that Being lying beyond the cosmos who himself is somehow the mysterious source of this destructive power operating in the universe, is able to dissolve this negative force by absorbing it back into himself. This Cosmic Being who is both the source of this poison and also the one who can absorb it back into himself is Siva. When Siva swallows this poison, his throat turns blue and hence he is known as 'NILAKANTHA'. 'Blue Throated'. After this it was possible for the cosmic principles of life of Devas and Asuras to receive the great gift of eternal life, which before had been too much for them and threatened to destroy them.

Man is a conscious being. He lives consciously. He acts consciously. It is in man's conscious experience that there is a struggle going on within himself and around him. This is the experience of man in the past as well as today. From the beginning of human history man began to ask himself, "What is this struggle? Why is this struggle? Who are these two forces in me fighting each other? What are they fighting for? Who are they? Where do they come from and where am I going?" The history of religion will tell us how man was to go on finding answers to these questions.

Man realizes that there are these mysterious forces in his fathomless consciousness. His experience shows his own limitations and mortality. Being a conscious being, man sees that there is this mysterious hidden power in the sub-conscious or unconscious levels. This hidden mysterious power of the unconscious is the gift of eternal life — Amrita. Man sees that if he could bring this Amrita into the conscious level, he will have eternal life, he will transcend all his limitations, he will enter into the eternal bliss where there is no more pain, suffering, hunger, thirst or death. Man's struggle in this world is to awaken this force from the unconscious and bring it to the conscious level. This is what the mythology of the churning of the cosmic ocean means. The cosmic ocean is the symbol of the sea of consciousness. But man realizes his limitations and powerlessness to churn the sea of consciousness. And also his limited consciousness is powerless to absorb the first drop of cosmic life or eternal life, because it is too powerful and too big. The first drop of Amrita is poison for man. In itself it is not poison but for man it is, because it is too powerful. For the mind of the ancients, poison is essentially what cannot be absorbed because it is too powerful, too big. It really shows man's experience of his limitation. Here man recognizes God's intervention in his life.

The mysterious, destructive and re-creative power lying hidden in man's fathomless consciousness is called Lord Siva. Siva is the Cosmic Being. He is the Cosmic Consciousness from whom we receive our consciousness. He is the eternal life-giving force. He is in the fathomless consciousness of man. The Kundalini Shakti, the power of Siva, is at the same time destructive and recreative, poison and Amrita. Siva is the God of the new creation. The homeopathic significance of the destructive power of Siva, is symbolised by the serpent. The poison of the serpent is creative and life-giving. In homeopathy it is believed that poison can be cured by poison which is connected with a mythical understanding of the good serpent (Nalla Pambu), who is both poisonous and healing. Various parts of the snake are thought to cure ailments in village and tribal folk-lore, and in fact the serpent itself is often the guarantee of wholeness and consequently health. The sign of the snake in sexual congress, on the snake-stones beneath the tree, is not only a fertility symbol, but it is the same as used in the cults of Aesculapius and still employed as a symbol of medicine. The figure of the serpent which was raised in the desert by Moses was to cure the Hebrews of snake-bite, and thus a holy serpent, or python, is raised in order to take upon itself, like Siva, the poison of the world. "Moses made a bronze serpent, and set it on a pole, and if a serpent bit any man, he would look at the bronze serpent and live" (Num. 21:9). The serpent on the cross is the medical symbol for healing. "As Moses lifted up the serpent in the wilderness, so must the Son of Man be lifted up, that whoever believes in him have eternal life" (Jn. 3:14). Here Jesus, the Son of Man on the Cross, is symbolized as a bronze serpent on a pole, as symbol of healing power, eternal life giving force.

The collective unconscious is symbolized by the serpent. Siva, being the hidden force of the unconscious and the force which generates the poison to recreate man and the cosmos through destruction, enters into the Cosmic Consciousness of man and takes into himself the poison of the world and makes it possible for men, the cosmic principles of life and darkness, Devas and Asuras, to receive the gift of eternal life which before was too much for them and threatened to destroy them. This hidden force lying in the unconscious state of man is poison as well as Amrita. When Siva swallowed the poison it gave rise to a colour, the colour of blue, that is to say, it stained the conscious mind and left behind in the invisible conscious world its mark. This was a sort of initiation into eternal life.

The consciousness of God becomes the consciousness of man, in the form of Siva. Cosmic principles of light and darkness, Devas and Asuras, are the two natures of man. In and through Siva Consciousness, man is able to absorb the poison and Amrita, that means, the destruction of the old consciousness and the recreation of the new consciousness, his death to the individual body consciousness and life to Cosmic Consciousness of Siva. Siva initiates us into the process of death and life as a means to grow in Cosmic Consciousness. This growth in higher consciousness is the process of evolution. The whole cosmos is growing to, moving to its fulness in Siva Consciousness. Man is the center of the cosmos and the Cosmic Consciousness. The growth in higher consciousness is the experience of man.

Siva stands as the Lord of integration or wholeness. He is the Lord of the cosmos. This harmony of the cosmos, the heaven and earth, is represented by the cosmic dance of Siva. "Siva dances in the graveyard stepping over the god of lust (the graveyard and the god of lust represent man's state of disharmony and mortality) and because of this cosmic dance the whole cosmos sustains its existence and rhythmic movement. The whole cosmos is dancing and moving to its fulness in 'saccidananda' — truth, consciousness and bliss". What we have to do is allow ourselves to be moved by this rhythmic movement of the Cosmic Consciousness through the process of evolution, destruction and recreation, death and life, ascending and descending.

CONCLUSION

Man's experience of the mysterious supernatural power hidden in him is expressed through the symbolism of the serpent at the foot of the tree, coiled around the navel of the cosmos, lying in the depths of the ocean, sleeping in the unconscious or fathomless consciousness of man, lying coiled at the base of the spine of man. Perhaps all religions which have evolved the concept of a really personal God, Bhaghvan (Lord of the womb), have emerged out of a tradition in which serpents have been extremely important symbols of the supernatural. The serpent deities were worshipped and believed in in the Pre-Aryan religions not as personal gods, but rather, as the presiding genus of the field or home, or the very inner psyche of man; a sort of eternal, natural, indwelling Lord. Krishna's battle with the serpent-tribe that inhabited the holy river, near Brindavan, has a symbolic meaning of overthrowing the Pre-Aryan serpent worship.

2. *Evolution of Man's Experience of the Supernatural Power from Cosmic Serpent to Cosmic Man Jesus Christ*

In the mind of Christians there is a deep-rooted aversion towards the serpent. They will find it extremely difficult to accept the serpent as the symbol of supernatural power, as something positive and good. In the Bible the serpent is symbolized as the embodiment of demoniac power — the symbol of evil. (2 Kg. 18:4; Gen. 49:17; to 20:14; Ps. 58:5; Prov. 22:32 etc.) The Hebrew had a natural aversion for the snake, intensified by the fact that it was the object of worship in Canaan. From the excavations at Batshain, Geser, Tanah, etc., it is beyond question that the snake was not only a phallic symbol connected with the mother goddess, but also an emblem of the occult — knowledge linked with magic and divination. The serpent was the symbol of fertility and superhuman knowledge. In later Judaism and the New Testament the snake or dragon is the personification of the devil (Wis. 2:24; Apoc. 12:9, 22; Enoch 69:6). "There was war in heaven, Michael and the angels under his command fought the dragon and his host of fallen angels. And the dragon lost the battle and was forced from heaven. This great dragon, the ancient serpent called the satan, the one deceiving the whole world, was thrown down into the earth with all his army" (Rev. 12:29). "The furious dragon sent out to attack the rest of her children — all who were keeping God's commandments — and confessing that they belong to Jesus. He stood waiting on an ocean beach" (Rev. 12:17).

"So the Lord God said to the serpent: 'This is your punishment. You are singled out from among all the domestic and wild animals of the whole earth — to be cursed. You shall grovel in the dust as long as you live, crawling along on your belly. From now on you and the woman will be enemies, as well as all of your offspring and hers. And I will put the fear of you into the woman, and between your offspring and hers.

She shall strike you on your head, while you will strike at her heel'."

How did the serpent become the personification of the devil in the Old Testament as well as in the New Testament? It is because Yahweh became the personal God of Israel. All other deities became enemies and were looked upon as enemies. So the serpent deity was replaced by Yahweh. "I am Yahweh your God who liberated you from your slavery in Egypt. You may worship no other god than me. You shall not make yourselves any idols, any images resembling animals, birds or fish. You must never bow to an image or worship it in any way, for I, the Lord your God, am very possessive. I will not share your affection with any other god" (Ex. 20:1-5).

In the primitive religions of the world, as we already know, the serpent is the symbol of man's experience of the supernatural power. The serpent deities are worshipped and believed in not as personal gods but rather as the presiding genius of the field or home, or the very inner psyche of man, as a sort of elemental, natural, indwelling Lord. According to the evolution of man from the life in the forest to the civilized world, his understanding and experience of the supernatural power, or God, also was growing. In the primitive religion man depended on nature and its various forces, sun, moon, stars, sky, rains, ocean, wind, trees, mountains, rocks and animals.

Man depended on sun because the sun gave light and energy so he had to please the sun for his existence. Honour, worship and rituals were given to the sun and the sun became the Sun God. The sun is the symbol of man's experience of the supernatural power as light and energy. Man has to depend on rain for his existence and thus the rain god evolves. Similarly the various forces of nature became gods. There are innumerable gods and goddesses through whom man experienced the supernatural power. There was a time when man fully depended on trees for his livelihood and shelter so the tree became the center of his life and worship. These various forces of nature, the sun, moon, stars, heaven, earth, waters, mountains, trees, rocks, animals, birds, etc., have a double function in man's life. They do good to man as well as harm to man. Without them the life of man is impossible and at the same time they destroy the life of man. For example; the wind brings rain and if there is too much wind it will destroy everything. Take the serpent — every part of the serpent is medicinal. The poison of the serpent in its minute quantity is medicinal, it gives life to man, but if he is bitten by the serpent he will die. Like this anything in the creation will have a double function, a good and bad effect on man. Since man experiences the supernatural power of God through these various forces of nature which have good and bad effect on man, man experienced and believed that this double effect, good and bad, ultimately comes from the supernatural power of God. God is the source and everything comes from him. God destroys man and he saves man. God gives life and death to man. God works through destruction and recreation. These experiences of death and life, the homeopathic salvific work of God, are experienced and symbolized by the serpent in the primitive religion. When man recognized Yahweh as the personal God, the God of salvation, the impersonal force of God, the serpent was looked down on. Here we can see a growth in man's experience of the supernatural power from serpent to Yahweh. From the point of view of man, when we look at it, we see that experience of God is growing and is taking a new shape. In God there is absolutely no change. God remains ever the same. He is neutral beyond good and bad. But man sees God's innumerable ways and forms. The intervention of God in man's life is experienced as destructive and re-creative. We see Yahweh, the God of Israel, manifested himself not only as the God of justice, the God of mercy, but also as an angry God, a God of destruction and a God of thunder and lightning. The Lord says to Israel "My wrath may burn hot against them and I may consume them" (Ex. 32:10). All through the scripture we see the fight between Yahweh and the serpent god, between the people who accepted Yahweh as their God of salvation and the people who still continue to believe the serpent deity as their God of salvation. In the Paradise story we see that Yahweh says to Adam, "You should not eat the fruit of the tree" and the serpent comes and says, "If you eat the fruit you will become like God". This is an expression of the conflict between Yahweh and the serpent deity. This fight is not just because the serpent deity is the symbol of evil and Yahweh is the symbol of God. In themselves both the serpent deity and Yahweh stand for the supernatural power. The conflict is in man, the fight is in man; the enmity and hatred are in man; good and bad effects are in man; but man projects all that he experiences in himself on God in whom he believes. All through the history of various religions we can see this fight going on, between Jewish religion and Gentile religion, Jews and Christians, Christians and Muslims, Christians and Hindus in the name of their respective gods. Is it because one god is evil and the other god is good? From the beginning of humanity till now the war is going on, one nation against another nation. Millions and millions of people are being killed. Is it because one nation is good and the other nation is evil? Through the natural calamities millions of people are being killed, the flood, drought, thunder, cyclone, earthquake. Is it because they are evil? Is the flood evil? Is the cyclone evil? The good and bad effects come from the same source. In itself everything is beyond good and evil. But when it operates in man the double effect comes, good and bad effects.

In the primitive religion the serpent is the symbol of the supernatural power and the natural power. When the supernatural power is separated from the natural power the natural power becomes the contrary force to the supernatural power. The natural power becomes the enemy or evil. Evil is the absence of reality. When the supernatural power is separated from the natural power, it becomes the absence of the supernatural power. The natural power in the absence of the supernatural power becomes evil and it is personified as devil. In this sense the serpent which is the symbol of supernatural and natural power, when it is separated from the supernatural, the serpent becomes the symbol of natural power and the symbol of the devil. In the Bible Yahweh is symbolized as the personification of the supernatural power and the serpent is the symbol of the devil. In the New Testament this is also followed. Jesus is the symbol of the supernatural power and the serpent is the symbol of the devil. We see all through the Bible, in the Old and New Testament, the fight between these two forces. It is the conflicts in man between the divine and human, between the supernatural and the natural power, the purusha and prakrati.

The Christian Yogic experience of the serpent is not as the personification of evil but rather man's experience of the supernatural power operating in him, and he undergoes the experience of death and life. The serpent gives death to man and also life to man. The serpent is the symbol of God's homeopathic work of salvation. The poison of the serpent is destructive and re-creative.

This understanding of the serpent will help us to understand Yahweh the God of Israel. The salvific work of Yahweh too is homeopathic through destruction and re-creation. The one who believes in Yahweh will undergo the experience of death and life. Man's experience of Yahweh's intervention in his life is destructive and at the same time re-creative. Man experienced Yahweh as God of wrath, God of redemption, God of anger and God of mercy. The experience of Job is a very good example.

The understanding of the serpent will help us to understand the Son of Man, Jesus Christ, the servant of Yahweh. The salvific work of Jesus too is homeopathic, through destruction and re-creation. The Paschal Mystery, death and life, is the symbol of this homeopathic salvific work of Jesus Christ. "If anyone wants to follow me, let him deny himself and take up his cross". "Unless you drink this cup you will not have eternal life". To drink the cup means to drink the poison, but it gives both death and life.

3. *Paradise*

There was not a paradise the way we were taught and the way we understand and the way we read in the Bible. Then what type of paradise was there? It will be answered by a counter question. Is there a paradise today? If there is a paradise today, then there was a paradise then, too. What is my experience today? What is the experience of the people today? All would agree that there is struggle going on in man and his society. There is a force which pulls me down all the time, and there is a force which raises me up. I want to do something and I am not able to fulfil it. I desire one thing and something else happens. I want to grow as an integral personality, but my senses fall short. My senses are carried away with the material world. Man experiences that there is this hidden mysterious force in him and he is unable to awaken it. Today we experience suffering, pain and disharmony, and the inability to come out of it. Man wants to come out of chaos to cosmos, from disharmony to harmony. Man is looking forward to a better world, a better living condition, where there is no more pain or sorrow, a peaceful and pleasant life. There are these two feelings of man, one is his experience of limitation and the other is his expectation.

The moment man became a conscious being he began to experience consciously. According to the theory of evolution man was gradually evolving into a conscious being and he is still evolving into his perfection. As soon as man became a conscious being, he began to experience his limitations and powerlessness and at the same time there was this deep desire in him to become perfect. The experience of his limitation, mortality and powerlessness and the desire to transcend all his limitations, mortality and powerlessness began to grow side by side according to the development and evolution of his consciousness. Once man evolved as a conscious being he began to realize that there is a mysterious hidden force in his fathomless consciousness. His normal consciousness has not enough power to awaken and receive these forces.

In this state of consciousness man is in need of a super

consciousness or super being to awaken his fathomless consciousness. Man began to depend on various forces around him in the universe as well as on the forces in himself. These various forces inside and outside of him, which he considered greater than himself, became deities and the focus of worship. By pleasing these deities man received their assistance and favours. In the process of man's evolution and the development of his consciousness, Yahweh replaces the serpent deity and becomes the God of Israel. Israel experienced Yahweh's intervention in their lives as saviour and redeemer. Yahweh promised to the people of Israel a land, a new society where there is no more pain and suffering — a perfect harmony. The people of Israel experienced the power of Yahweh liberating them, re-creating them, bringing perfect order and harmony from chaos to cosmos. In the light of Yahweh's intervention and promises, to the Israelites came to the consciousness of their condition, in which they were in a state of chaos and they looked forward to the promised land — a perfect, peaceful, harmonious nation. And in the light of the expectation promised by Yahweh, they looked back and projected this expectation of the paradise as the original state. The paradise which we read of in the Genesis story is a symbolic expression of the paradise which the Israelites were desiring to achieve in the future. So, in reality there was not a paradise in the way we see in Genesis. It was an imagination of the future reality. This paradise must be understood in the light of Israel's experience of Yahweh's intervention as saviour.

At the same time the Israelites experienced the power of Yahweh awakening them and re-creating them through suffering and the experience of death, they began to experience little by little paradise, eternal life, peace and harmony. Yahweh's salvific work followed the pattern of evolution. The Israelites were gradually growing in the higher consciousness and experience of Yahweh's intervention. In this sense man began to experience the paradise from the moment he became a conscious being. Suffering, death, disharmony — and paradise, peace and harmony. Israelites were experiencing both from the moment they became conscious of Yahweh's intervention.

All through the history of Israel, we see they were looking forward to a perfect life, immortal life. They looked for a Messiah. In the process of evolution Jesus comes and places himself in the place of Yahweh and the serpent.

In the Old Testament the Israelites experienced Yahweh as the saviour and in the New Testament Jesus becomes the saviour. "As Moses in the wilderness lifted up the bronze image of a serpent on a pole, even so I (Son of Man) must be lifted upon a pole so that everyone who believes in me will have eternal life." Jesus comes as the eternal life-giving force. Jesus through his death and resurrection brings forth creation into its fullness.

In Jesus man reaches the climax of his evolution. Man enters into the super consciousness of Christ, and there he experiences the new heaven, new earth, new Jerusalem, a new city, a new creation, a new kingdom, the Kingdom of God the Father, where there is no more suffering and pain. Man transcends his limitations and enters into eternal life. This new city is the paradise where things on earth and things in heaven are gathered together in unity in Christ. Christ is the head and the whole creation is his body. This is a reality which has to be fulfilled in the future experience.

The whole work of salvation, the fulfilment of the new creation in Christ, has to be seen in the process of evolution.

The Kingdom of God or paradise is at hand, already begun. It is with us, but it is a dynamic reality which is in the process of evolving to its fulfilment. Death and life is the process of evolution and growth of the whole world in Christ.

Like the first humanity, we too, today, experience our limitations, mortality, suffering, pain, hatred, enmity, disharmony, powerlessness, etc. At the same time we experience in Christ the eternity, immortality, joy, peace, love, harmony, power, etc., as a future reality present in us which is going to be fulfilled at the parousia. In and through Christ Consciousness, when I look back in the light of the future hope, I can see a paradise which was existing from the beginning of creation, but as a dynamic reality growing to its perfection in Christ at parousia.

4. *Christian Yogic Experience of the Kundalini Shakti Yoga in the Light of the Story of Paradise*

Paradise is a mode of man's experience when everything is harmony. It is the experience of Yogic consciousness, the union between man and man, union between man and nature, union between man and God, union between heaven and earth. Everything is totally integrated. There are three main symbols that are used in the paradise story — Adam, the tree of life and the serpent. *Adam represents mankind.* The tree is the symbol of man's experience of death and life as the process of evolution or growth. The tree is the symbol of the mystical marriage between heaven and earth, between God and man. *In brief, the tree is the symbol of man.* The serpent is the symbol of the supernatural and natural power identified or the divine and human power identified one with the other.

God tells Adam, you should not eat the fruit of this particular tree. The tree in the middle of the garden stands for God. The fruit stands for the will of God. Instead of God standing there, the tree or the fruit is there. Man ate the fruit. That means he ate the will of God. He ate God. The temptation was if you eat the fruit you will become like God. Man ate the fruit and became God. He ate the author of life. Now man is everything. He centered on himself. Beyond him there is nothing. There is no more God for him because he substituted himself for God. He lost the vision of God. He depended fully on himself. God sent man out of the garden. He lost the harmony between heaven and earth. There is no more heaven for him. Earth is everything for him. This world became his kingdom. God asked man, who told you to eat the fruit. The man replied, the woman whom you gave me as companion gave me the fruit and the woman said the serpent gave it for me. Here already is a division between man and woman. Now everything is in chaos. Disharmony between man and man, man and woman, man and nature, man and God, heaven and earth, divine and human. Man entered into earth-centered state, ego-centered state, death state, ignorant state. This is the Yogic understanding of sin and death.

What happened to the serpent? God said to the serpent, go down to the earth and roll on the ground. Walk with your belly and eat the dust of the earth. In the paradise when the serpent was on top of the tree, the supernatural and natural power, the divine and human power were in harmony. When the divine power is cut away from the natural power the serpent lost its balance and within a second it fell down to the foot of the tree.

In paradise when the serpent is on the top of the tree or at the top of the head of man, it symbolises that the supernatural and natural power are in harmony and it is the sign of enlightenment or awakened state. When the serpent is at the foot of the tree or at the base of the spine of man, it symbolises that the supernatural and natural power are in disharmony and it is the sign of an ignorant or sleeping state. It means the supernatural power is identified with the natural power, hidden in man in a very mysterious way as a serpent coiled at the base of the spine. This is what is meant by saying that God is sleeping in man. He is hidden in man. This is what the power of the unconscious means; the serpent at the base of the spine or foot of the tree is the symbol of the power of the unconscious. The serpent at the top of the head or on the tree is the symbol of the power of the conscious or super consciousness. When man was in paradise the serpent was at the top of his head. In the fallen man, the serpent is coiled at the base of his spine.

What happened to the tree of life? The tree of life became the tree of death. The living tree became the dead tree. The leaves and branches dried and fell off till it became a dead cross. The tree, when it was a living tree of paradise, was the symbol of life and knowledge of good and harmony. Now this tree became the symbol of death and knowledge of evil. This dead tree became the tree of the cross, symbolising the fallen humanity under the dominion of death. In paradise man experienced the serpent as life-giving nectar 'Amritam'. In the fallen state man experiences the serpent as death, poison.

The evil or sin in fallen humanity is that ego-centered state, the total dependence on man's own physical, mental and psychic power and total denial of a divine power beyond himself. Man himself is his own glory. Man's total vision of reality is closed up in his scientific achievements. Beyond his reach there is nothing. Man is God for himself. He is closed up to the reality of life. He is dead to the reality of life. The human power, which separated from the divine power, created a world of its own, where man is the center of everything. There is nothing beyond this world.

In the paradise story, the serpent can be symbolised as the natural power separated from the supernatural power and in that sense the serpent is the personification of evil. In the paradise story, Yahweh is the personificiation of the supernatural or divine power and the serpent is the personification of the natural or human power. In fallen humanity, these two powers are in conflict. And this is the chaos, the disharmony.

Jesus Christ the son of Man comes to this world as second Adam. He went into the state where fallen humanity was. Jesus takes into himself the fallen human nature, the serpent coiled at the base of the fallen man, the serpent at the foot of the dead tree of the Cross. As a serpent, he climbs the dead tree, the Cross, through the experience of death by drinking the poison of death, the poison of the serpent, the cup of salvation and reaches to the top of the tree, of the Cross. And the word of the scripture is thus fulfilled, "As Moses in the wilderness lifted up the image of a bronze serpent, on a pole, even so I must be lifted upon a pole so that anyone who believes in me will have eternal life." Again, the tree of death became the tree of life, the serpent on the Cross is the symbol of Jesus Christ, the Son of Man on the Cross. It means that the serpent is on the top of the head of the Son of Man, Jesus Christ.

The whole cosmos is moving towards its perfection by the cosmic dance of Jesus Christ the Son of Man on the Cross. The harmony between heaven and earth, divine and human power, God and man is restored. Jesus invites every man to enter into eternal life. "If anyone wants to follow me, let him deny himself and take up the Cross." "Unless you drink this cup you will not have eternal life." The Paschal Mystery of death and life is the symbol of this homeopathic salvific work of Jesus Christ. The serpent is the symbol of eternal life. The first drop of the poison of the serpent is the experience of death, and the second drop is the experience of life. Like the serpent on the tree, Jesus is on the Cross, inviting us to come and drink from him. "I am the eternal life-giving water, Amrita. And whoever drinks will have eternal life". But first it will taste as poison and then as Amrita.

As a Christian Yogi, when I look into myself, into my fathomless consciousness, I experience the indwelling presence of the power of Jesus Christ, the Risen Lord, as a serpent lying coiled at the base of the spine in a very mysterious hidden way. My Christian Yogic practice is to allow this power to pass through various centers of my body to the top of the head and take possession of me and unite me with the Heavenly Father. When the Spirit of Jesus takes possession of me, I will burn in the fire of Christ and experience death and thus enter into eternal life.

This process of enlightenment by the power of the Risen Lord Jesus Christ takes place in me as a gradual process, not as a sudden static action but as a dynamic reality. The Risen Lord Jesus Christ is the Cosmic Man who is this mysterious hidden force moving the cosmos, the whole of humanity, to its fulfilment at the parousia through the process of evolution, through the process of destruction and recreation, death and life. He is the head and the whole creation is his body. Things on earth and things in heaven gathered together in unity in Christ. He is the past, present and future. He is the beginning and the end.

5. *The Seven Chakras*

In Kundalini Yoga, the entire concentration is in one's own body. In our body there are seven major chakras. The chakras are the nerve centers or psychic centers or spiritual centers in our body. By concentrating on the chakras while breathing in and breathing out, one awakens the physical, mental, psychic and spiritual forces which are sleeping or hidden in these centers. In most people, these psychic centers are lying dormant and inactive, and much of man's potential is not utilised. Modern psychology agrees with yogic philosophy that man normally uses not more than a tenth of the available capacity in the brain, likewise there are almost infinite unknown depths within our subconscious and unconscious minds about which we know little. By conscious breathing and other yogic practices the subconscious and unconscious minds get integrated with the conscious mind and thus the conscious mind grows into super consciousness. By concentrating on the chakras, while doing asanas, pranayama or meditation, the energy is stimulated to flow to the chakras. It will help to awaken the corresponding faculties in the psychic and spiritual bodies, and will allow the individual to experience levels of consciousness, of which he is normally unaware.

The seven main chakras are located in the region of the spinal cord, from the lowest point in the perineum to the top of the head.

a. MOOLADHARA CHAKRA (Root center, Moola = root; adhara = place)

Mooladhara is the lowest chakra at the base of the spine. Mooladhara is the root center where the most primal energy the Kundalini Shakti is seated. Kundalini is in the form of a serpent in deep sleep, coiled in this center. It is the source of all energy in man and the universe, whether expressed as sexual, emotional, mental, psychic or spiritual energies. The natural and supernatural power is in union in a very mysterious way hidden within us at the base of the spine — the Mooladhara Chakra. This power is called the Kundalini Shakti. This power is also called the power of the unconscious. In this chakra, God is experienced as the source of everything, as the source of all energies, as the creator of the universe. This power is experienced by Christian Yogis as the indwelling presence of the Holy Spirit, the power of the Risen Lord, Jesus Christ, the Cosmic Man.

b. SWADHISTHANA CHAKRA (one's own abode, swa = self; sthan = dwelling place)

Swadhisthana Chakra is a little above the Mooladhara, just behind the genital organ. This is the sex center through which one enters into reproductive activity. It is through this center that one experiences God as the source of reproduction and maintenance. By opening this center one awakens the sexual energies.

c. MANIPURA CHAKRA (city of Jewels, Mani = Jewels; Pura = city)

Manipura Chakra is situated at the navel. It is the center for heat and vitality. It is the fire center of our body. The whole body receives energy from this center. It is this fire which digests food. It is through this center one realizes God as a fire which destroys one's own body and the whole universe in order to re-create.

d. ANAHATA CHAKRA (unstruck, an = not; ahat = struck)

Anhata Chakra is located in the heart. Vibrations or sounds are produced in the universe by striking objects together. In our body the vibrations or sounds are produced by the heartbeat. Behind the heartbeat there is another sound or vibration. Once the Anahata Chakra is opened one is able to perceive the unstruck sound, unborn or undying vibration. Through this chakra one experiences God as eternal vibration. This is what the mystics experience in the cave of the heart as the inner voice of God.

e. VISHUDDHI CHAKRA (Vishuddhi = purity)

The Vishuddhi Chakra is located in the throat. Vishuddhi means purity. It is the center for purification. It is in this center that the Yogis taste the divine nectar Amrita. The psalmist says, "taste and see how God is." In the Vishuddhi Chakra God is expressed as the eternal life-giving nectar. The first taste of Amrita is bitter (poison) which gives death and purification and then follows the taste of Amrita sweet which gives life. A Christian Yogi tastes the body and blood of Christ as the eternal life-giving nectar which too tastes at first bitter (poison) and gives experience of death, and then sweet, giving experience of life.

f. AJNA CHAKRA (Ajna = command)

Ajna Chakra is located at the point between the eyebrows Bhrumadhyam. Ajna means command. It is through this center that the disciple receives command and instruction from the Master. Once this center is opened one will be able to discern the truth, one will be able to recognize the right teacher and right teaching. Ajna Chakra is called the third eye, the eye of wisdom. Through the third eye one sees the divine light and in that light the vision of reality.

g. SAHASRARA (thousand petals)

Sahasrara means the thousand petal lotus. It is located at the top of the head. This center is the abode of the highest consciousness. It is in this center that the divine and the human power unite together. It is in this center that the marriage between Purusha and Prakrita, the male and female, takes place. It is in this center that the marriage between heaven and earth, God and man, unconscious mind and the conscious mind takes place.

6. *Technique of Kundalini Shakti Meditation*

a. FIRST STAGE

While breathing in become aware of the movement from the Mooladhara Chakra at the base of the spine to the

Sahasrara at the top of the head. Let the mind flow with the movement of the breath from the Mooladhara Chakra to Sahasrara. Breathing in begins from the Mooladhara and ends at Sahasrara. The mind flows with the movement of the breath through all the chakras one after the other from the base of the spine to the top of the head.

While breathing out become aware of the movement from the Sahasrara, the top of the head, to the Mooladhara, the base of the spine. Let the mind flow with the movement of the breath from Sahasrara to the Mooladhara Chakra. Breathing out begins from Sahasrara and ends at Mooladhara Chakra. The mind flows with the movement of the breath through all the chakras one after the other from the top of the head to the base of the spine.

While breathing in become aware of the mantra Yē (Yeshu) and while breathing out Ā (Abba). Listen to the subtle vibration while breathing in and breathing out. While breathing in and out the concentration is not on the nostril but inside the body. The vibration of the breath can be felt in the gap while breathing in and out. It is not the same type of Mahat Yoga Pranayama as we did in the previous technique. Here we don't give any attention to the expansion of the abdomen, mid-chest and upper chest areas. And in fact we don't see externally any expansion of the lungs. The entire concentration is inside. From the outside appearances it is as if you are not breathing. But of course the same amount of air passes through the lungs as in the previous technique. This is interior Mahat Yoga Pranayama (Andheriya Pranayama). The other one was extension pranayama (Bahya Pranayama)

Begin with deep and long breathing. The timing of the breathing will vary during the meditation. For example, 6:6;

5:5; 4:4; 2:2; 1:1. Sometimes the breathing will be very long and sometimes very short. But the mind and the mantra must flow with the prana — the vital force.

b. SECOND STAGE

While breathing in from Mooladhara Chakra become aware of the mysterious hidden presence of God through the Holy Spirit. God, who is immanent in man, manifests himself through the Holy Spirit as the mysterious supernatural power. Mooladhara Chakra is symbolized as the seat of the hidden force in man. It is the seat of the unconscious. God is present in the fathomless consciousness of man. While breathing in from Mooladhara man undergoes the experience of the awakening of God within. From his fathomless unconscious man undergoes the experience and transformation when God awakens from Mooladhara. Man undergoes within him consciously the effect of the whole revelation of God. The Christian Yogic experience of the revelation of God is from the Father to the Son, Jesus, through the Holy Spirit.

The Yogic understanding of God begins as the transcendent God who is immanent in man in his fathomless unconscious, 'the Mooladhara Chakra.' God the Father from the Mooladhara Chakra, from the fathomless unconscious, from the ultimate source, breathes out himself through the Spirit as Word. From the Word, the whole creation, the whole of humanity, Jesus Christ, the Son of Man, comes forth. In the fullness of time Jesus Christ, the Son of Man, returns to God the Father as the Risen Lord, the Lord of the universe, as the Cosmic Christ, as the head of the whole creation. As Christian Yogis we can experience the whole revelation of God the Father within our bodies through the seven chakras which are the physical, mental, psychic and spiritual centers in the human body. The seven chakras are the seven levels of consciousness in which man experiences the manifold manifestations or revelations of God who is ultimately beyond forms, names and qualities, and also the fullness of forms and qualities.

In the Mooladhara Chakra, God is revealed as creator who is named Brahma in Hinduism and God the Father in Christianity. God the Father creates the universe, creates conscious man from the sea of consciousness, from the fathomless consciousness which is the supreme consciousness of God the Father. The Christian Yogic experience of this consciousness of God the Father is his Word. The Word is the mind or will of God the Father. The supreme consciousness of God the Father manifests in its fulness in His Son Jesus Christ, the Word, and the supreme consciousness of God the Father, incarnates in Jesus Christ, the Cosmic Man.

God the Father is fully present in Jesus Christ the Cosmic Man. The whole universe is present in Jesus Christ, as St. Paul puts it, Christ is the head and the whole creation is his body. The whole of mankind and the universe, Jesus Christ and God the Father, are very mysteriously present in the Holy Spirit. The Holy Spirit, as the mysterious force dwelling in the Mooladhara Chakra, reveals this mystery.

While breathing in from the Mooladhara receive this mysterious hidden force, the Holy Spirit, through the natural vital force, the prana. The Holy Spirit, through the breath, reveals the Son Jesus Christ and in the Son Jesus Christ, God the Father as the creator of the universe.

In brief, in the Mooladhara Chakra, God is revealed as the Holy Spirit, the mysterious hidden force of the unconscious.

This mysterious supernatural force is symbolized as the Kundalini Shakti, the Serpent Power.

7. *How to Use the Sexual Energy in Kundalini Shakti Yoga*

During the Kundalini Shakti Yoga meditation, this mysterious force awakens as a serpent from the Mooladhara Chakra. From the Mooladhara Chakra, the Kundalini Shakti arises to the Swadhisthana Chakra and awakens the sexual energies. Once the sexual energies are awakened, how to handle them? Normally what religious people do when the sexual energies are awakened is to regard it as the temptation of the devil and start mortifying the body to overcome the temptation; or suppress the feelings, or jump into action in order to satisfy the senses. But there is another way which is yogic and physically, mentally, psychologically and spiritually healthy.

a. THE FIRST TYPE OF PRACTICE

When St. Benedict was meditating in Subiaco cave in Italy, one day uncontrollable sexual energies were awakened in him. He recognized it as a temptation of the devil to turn him off from the spiritual path. St. Benedict lived in the time when the religious people believed that the world and flesh were something profane, an obstacle for spiritual life. Anything related to the flesh such as sex and sexual feelings tended to be regarded as evil. Sexual feelings were very often identified with temptation of the devil. In this time the philosophical understanding was of man as body and soul. The goal of life was to set the soul free from the body, so that the soul leaves the body and unites with God, while the body in its present state is profane and belongs to the world and Satan. So the soul has a continuous fight with the body in order to be free from the temptation of the body. All the spiritual teachings are oriented towards this.

Now what did St. Benedict do when the sexual energy was awakened? He got up and went out of the cave and rolled among the thorns and mortified his body and overcame the temptation of sexual feelings. He distracted himself from the sexual feelings by mortifying his body. He used violence to his body to overcome the temptation.

b. THE SECOND TYPE OF PRACTICE

Very often religious people suppress the sexual feelings when it is awakened. We suppress all the sexual feelings and emotions because it is something evil and an obstacle or temptation in spiritual life. We will not allow the sexual feelings to come up and manifest themselves. This type of practice led many religious, especially the Catholic nuns and priests and brothers, into physical, mental and psychological sickness. As we know today there are many psychological therapies to heal people of this sickness.

c. THE THIRD TYPE OF PRACTICE

When the sexual energies are awakened immediately jump into action, such as intercourse, masturbation, or emission of semen, or any action in order to satisfy at once the sexual urges. This belongs more to the animal nature.

d. THE FOURTH TYPE IS YOGIC

As a Yogi who practices Kundalini Shakti Yoga according to the modern religious understanding, what should one do when the sexual energies are awakened while in meditation? When the sexual energies are awakened, I would say to myself something good is happening in me. Sex is not evil. Sexual feelings are not evil. It is not the temptation of the devil. The body or flesh is not evil. Whatever God created is good. The body and soul together makes a man. I cannot separate body from soul. They are inseparable. The ultimate state of man is not to leave the body behind so that the soul gets united with God. Rather, the total man, that is body and soul, unites with God. When the sexual energies are awakened, I just remain seated with full awareness experiencing what is happening in me. And I experience the flow of energy. Energy is not static. It moves, it flows from one chakra to another. In this state of awareness one can experience the flow of sexual energies from Swadhisthana Chakra to Manipura Chakra and then to all the other chakras till finally it reaches to the top of the head, the Sahasrara Chakra. When the sexual energy is awakened, one should not jump immediately into action, such as sexual intercourse or emission of semen or masturbation, etc. If one can just remain with the awareness one will have beautiful and blissful experiences of the flow of sexual energies from the Swadhisthana Chakra. It is God who is the source of these sexual energies who in a very mysterious way is hidden in the Mooladhara Chakra. We as Christian Yogis recognize Him as the Holy Spirit, the mysterious force of the Risen Lord Jesus Christ, the Cosmic Man; and this is Kundalini Shakti.

There are many other ways we can experience the flow of

sexual energies and its transformation. The sexual energies flow into Manipura Chakra and transform into fire energy and then as fire energy it flows into Anahata Chakra and transforms into vibrations or inner voice and is called love vibrations. Then as love vibration it flows into Vishuddhi Chakra and transforms into eternal life-giving nectar, Amrita and then as eternal life-giving nectar it flows into Ajna Chakra and transforms into Mahat Guru, the great Master or Lord or spirit of wisdom, and finally as Mahat Guru it flows into Sahasrara Chakra and transforms into super consciousness. Here human and divine consciousness enter into mystical marriage, it is the total integration of the natural and supernatural, or human and divine energies. From Sahasrata Chakra the pure energy, the harmonized energy, radiates to the whole body and transforms the whole person. And this transformed body radiates the pure energy to the whole world.

Another way of understanding is that the Kundalini Shakti manifests in Swadhisthana Chakra as sexual energy and the awakened sexual energy radiates from Swadhisthana to the whole body. Then the Kundalini Shakti manifests in Manipura Chakra as fire energy and the awakened fire energy radiates to the whole body. Then the Kundalini Shakti manifests in Anahata Chakra as love vibration and the awakened love vibration radiates to the whole body. Then the Kundalini Shakti manifests in Vishuddhi Chakra as eternal life-giving nectar and the awakened life-giving force radiates to the whole body. Then Kundalini Shakti manifests in Ajna Chakra as guiding spiritual force, the great Master, and the awakened wisdom force radiates to the whole body. Then finally the Kundalini Shakti manifests as the super consciousness and awakened supernatural force radiates to the whole body. And then the enlightenment takes place.

8. *Kundalini Shakti Awakens from Our Subconscious the Good and Bad Effects of the Past Karmic Actions*

When we look back into life, from our childhood onwards there are various things which happened in our life. There are various events which took place, sometimes frightening experiences, sometimes very nice experiences. There are various actions good and bad in our life. Many things happened inside and outside and around us; in our relation with parents, family, teachers, friends, etc. The effect of all these actions have gone into me. Everything is within me. Where is it? I don't know, but I know it is within me. The psychologist would say everything is in our subconscious. The emotions, feelings, desires, impressions, everything that we suppressed is in our subconscious. According to the Kundalini Shakti Yoga all the effects of good and bad actions, are stored up in the chakras, the nerve or psychic centers in our body. The awakened Kundalini Shakti when it passes through various chakras, awakens these stored up effects of our Karmas and brings these to the conscious mind. That means the Kundalini Shakti awakens everything from our subconscious and brings it to the conscious mind at the top of the head.

In the process of this awakening one undergoes various experiences, sometimes very frightening, sometimes very pleasant. Various types of symptoms will manifest in the body both pleasant and unpleasant. For example: A person is afraid of darkness from his childhood onwards. When he meditates the Kundalini Shakti awakens from the sub-conscious the suppressed fear and symptoms will appear, similar symptoms to those which he would experience when faced with the darkness, such as: the hair of his body rises, unrhythmic breathing follows, pain in the stomach, trembling of the body, dryness of the lips and throat. When these symptoms manifest in his body inside and outside he must remain in meditation with full awareness, experiencing what is happening in him. If he faces this moment consciously he will experience these symptoms arising and going away. From the death of these symptoms his consciousness gets strength. Then gradually he will be able to face the darkness and he will not be afraid of darkness. He is already liberated from the fear of darkness.

So the Kundalini Shakti awakens from the subconscious various types of tension due to fear, anger, etc. The symptoms are the manifestation of these tensions. Once we face consciously the death of these symptoms our consciousness and the nervous system become strong and the liberation of the whole person takes place.

When the spirit awakens various forces from the subconscious such as anger, aggression, violence, passions of sex, and fear, many people will find them extremely difficult to face. In certain cases one has to use some violent means to control one's own passions. One may have to mortify the body as St. Benedict, St. Francis of Assisi or St. John of the Cross did. That means use some psychological therapy with the help of some psychologist. Even sometimes one has to stop the meditation for a time. Use some means either negative or positive to release the tension, the uncontrollable energy.

a. THIRD STAGE OF THE MEDITATION

While breathing in, the Kundalini Shakti flows from the Mooladhara Chakra at the base of the spine to the Sahasrara Chakra at the top of the head and while breathing out the Shakti flows to the whole body from the head to toes. While breathing in receive the energy and while breathing out send the energy to the whole body. While breathing in receive love, joy and peace of the Holy Spirit and while breathing out send the love, joy and peace to the whole body.

b. FOURTH STAGE OF THE MEDITATION

While breathing in become aware of energy entering the whole body. While breathing out the energy goes out through the whole body. While breathing in love, joy, peace of the Spirit enters through the whole body. While breathing out love, joy, peace goes out through the whole body. In this stage we breathe in and out not through the nostrils nor from the base of the spine but through the whole body. That means the awareness is in the movement of the prana in the whole body while breathing in and out.

c. FIFTH STAGE OF THE MEDITATION

In this stage, the transformation of the whole body takes place. One enters into Cosmic Christ Body Consciousness. One experiences the whole cosmos as his body. This cosmic body which is the body of Cosmic Christ is the dwelling place of God the Father. Here one transcends the breathing and enters into the eternal movement within the Cosmic Body of Christ. This is the experience of the Trinitarian life of God. The movement of the breath will be between the Father and the Son in the Spirit. Thus one shares the inner life of God. Yogic experience of the inner life of God is a cosmic dance of the cosmic serpent, the Kundalini Shakti. The Kundalini Shakti, the cosmic serpent, keeping its tail on earth and head in heaven, enters into the eternal dance and expresses its love, joy and peace. Dance is an expression of a harmonious rhythmic movement of life which radiates love, joy and peace.

A Yogi is the one who lives in this consciousness, this harmony within himself, between man and man, and with nature and God. The cosmic dance of the cosmic serpent, the Kundalini Shakti, is the celebration of the celestial marriage, the marriage of the heaven and earth, God and man, the divine and human power, the supreme person, 'Purusha', and nature 'Prakriti', the male and female, Yahweh and Israel, Christ and the Church.

PART VIII

EXPERIENCE OF DEATH AND LIFE
THE WAY TO EXPERIENCE GOD

PART VIII

EXPERIENCE OF DEATH AND LIFE THE WAY TO EXPERIENCE GOD

How far one undergoes the experience of death so far one will be able to experience the life after death, the 'Charamapadam' state after death. The scripture says man cannot see God and live. The beatific vision, seeing God face to face, takes place only after death. That means man has to die in order to see God. Man is conditioned by time, matter and space. God is beyond time, matter and space. If man wants to see God he must transcend his limitations. He must enter into the state where God is in order to see him and experience him. Death is the means for man to transcend his limitation of time, matter and space.

All religions teach ways and means of how to undergo the experience of death. While we are in this body we can undergo the experience of death. What is the meaning of death? What do we mean by saying a person is dead? Death is a total detachment from this state where we are now. It is the detachment from the world we live, from people, from relatives, from wealth, from name and fame, from one's own physical body, from the world of the senses, from reasoning and thinking, etc . . . If a man lives totally detached from all these attachments, then it is equal to death.

People in general are afraid of death. Once my Guruji visited an old priest who was bedridden with a serious sickness in a hospital. He was at the point of death. Everybody knew that he would die at any moment. Guruji talked to him for a while and concluded the conversation with saying, "I will pray for a happy death for you." Oh! What! It was a shock for the old priest. He expected that all would pray for his rapid recovery from illness. He was afraid of his death. He did not want to die. Even in the worst situation people say it is better to die than live. In the depth of their heart they don't want to die.

Why is there a fear of death? There is the uncertainty about the state after death. We are told about the agony of death. I don't want to die but I have to die. The god of death comes and takes away my life. I will fight with death but finally death will win. I have to die but I don't want to die. Why do I say that I don't want to die? Because I want to live. What does it mean? I want to live. It means that I want to be in this state where I am now. Here living means attachment. I am attached to my own body, my ideas, my desires, my feelings, my pleasures, my name, fame, status, my sense activities. I am attached to people, my family, parents, friends, wealth, possessions. Death means separation or detachment from all these attachments. I don't want to die — that means I don't want to be detached, I want to live but I have to die. So there is a conflict in me between death and life, detachment and attachment. The conflict brings forth in me severe unbearable pain. It is the pain of death. The pain of death brings forth the fear of death. Attachment and fear of death brings forth disharmony in my whole person.

When Jesus was praying in the Garden he had to undergo the agony of death. His whole being was undergoing severe pain. He really underwent the conflict between death and life. In one sense there should not have been any conflict in him because he didn't have any attachment or fear of death. Since he was totally detached, death should have been a transcending point from time, matter and space. It should have been a joyful and peaceful event. As we saw, the cause for fear and pain of death is the attachment. There was no fear of death in Jesus and there was no disharmony in him. Then why did Jesus undergo the pain of death? Because Jesus was sitting in the Garden not as an individual person. The whole creation was present in him. The disharmony, suffering, pain, aggression, fear, injustice, attachment of the whole humanity was present in Jesus. Jesus consciously underwent the struggle, the pain between life and death, in his own body. And he reached a point where the agony of death was so severe, beyond his capacity to bear and he cried to God the Father. The Father did not take away the cup but gave him the strength to undergo the experience of death. The climax of the pain of death was on the Cross. Through the experience of death Jesus entered into eternal life. We are called to share with the process of death and life. Jesus says: "If anyone wants to follow me let him carry the Cross, let him renounce everything, let him renounce all his wealth, let him renounce his family and finally, lose himself. Unless a grain of wheat falls on the ground and dies it will not grow. Unless you die you will not enter the Kingdom of God."

If one is totally detached from all attachment and if one lives in this world as if one is dead to the world then the final death will be peaceful. Such a man has already experienced what is death and has a foretaste of the life after death through the practice of detachment, so there is no fear of death in him.

The death and life process is the sign of growth. It is the law of nature. Every moment in our body the cells are breaking down and the new cells are taking birth. Through this process of death and life we are growing. Death in itself is very painful, it is breaking of ourselves. The life itself is joyful, it is taking birth. Since pain of death and joy of life take place in the same moment it is well balanced. Consciously or unconsciously the death and life process takes place in every moment of our life. Man is a conscious being and the more he lives consciously the more he experiences the process of death and life.

Some people have said that they had an experience of God while they were looking at flowers. And other people saw a beautiful flower and they enjoyed it but they didn't have an experience of God. If one had the experience of God while looking at the flower, that means he underwent the experience of death; and the other one who didn't have the experience of God, that means he didn't undergo the experience of death. How does one undergo the experience of death or the pain of death while looking at the flower? For example, look at a beautiful flower. With the first look we will be attracted by the beauty, colour, the arrangements of the petals, the center of the flower, etc. We will get attached through our senses to the outside manifestations of the flower. It is something very pleasant for our senses. The most important part of the flower — the seed — is inside the flower which we don't see. If the flower is so beautiful, how much more beautiful is the seed for which the flower is an outer cover. We must break through the flower to reach the seed. To see the seed the flower dies. It is unpleasant for our senses. The senses were attached to the flower, to its beauty, colour, arrangments of the petals. That is destroyed.

God is present in the flower. If we want to see God in the flower, we must break through the flower as we did to see the seed. At the first look we see the flower, at the second look we will see the presence of God. One has to break one's senses, one has to go beyond the senses, one has to get through the senses to see the reality. At the first look we get attached to what is seen externally. At the second look we transcend the attachment. The transcending the attachment is the experience of death and it is very painful and very humiliating.

A man who believes only in himself and his own senses and his own abilities cannot accept the limitations of his senses, his achievements. Such a man cannot transcend his senses. Such a man will not be able to experience the ultimate reality. The man who experiences God in the flower undergoes the experience of death. That means he transcends the attachments of his senses and he is in the state of consciousness where he is seeing but not seeing, touching but not touching. When a man reaches this state of detachment he will be able to experience God in everything around him.

There is another type of experience of death. A man with a contagious disease is lying down on the roadside. A bad smell is coming out from his wounded body. He is a very ugly looking man. I go near to that person but the bad smell is coming out, that means I should not smell. It is very unpleasant for my eyes to look. If I go and touch that person I, too, will get his sickness. It is a sickness which is not curable and death is the result. If I respect myself and my senses, I should not go near. If I go near to this person it is dangerous for me. If I want to live, I must keep myself away from him. So I walk away respecting my own life.

Now, a nun goes that way and sees this person lying down on roadside. She immediately runs to him and carries him in her arms to the hospital and looks after him. She says as soon as she saw him she had an experience of God, she saw Christ in him. If she had an experience of God, surely she underwent the experience of death, the pain of death. For her too, it was an unpleasant sight; she too smelled the bad smell, she too knew it is a contagious disease. She died to her senses, she underwent the pain of death, she transcended her senses, then only she could see Christ in him. That means she was smelling but not smelling, seeing but not seeing, touching but not touching, reasoning but not reasoning. Through the experience of death, through the total detachment she entered into a state of consciousness where she experienced God in him and saw that he too is part of the Mystical Body of Christ as she is and the whole humanity as the children of God the Father.

God is present everywhere and if we want to experience his presence we have to transcend our senses, we have to undergo the detachment, the experience of death.

We are like a seed in the Kingdom of God which has to grow day by day through the process of death and life. This process of growth through death and life takes place in us consciously, we experience the love, joy and peace of the Kingdom of God.

PART IX

YOGIC CELEBRATION OF THE EUCHARIST

PART IX

YOGIC CELEBRATION OF THE EUCHARIST

The Eucharist is the celebration of the same mystery which is realised in meditation in the stillness of body and mind. In the Eucharistic celebration we experience the same reality and the same level of consciousness as in meditation but under signs, symbols, gestures and words. In meditation so far we were trying to transcend the senses, intellect, thoughts and words in order to enter into the stillness of the body and mind. But in the Eucharistic celebration we will use our intellect, senses, emotions, feelings, thoughts, words, etc. We will use all our faculties to express our experiennce of the Cosmic Christ Body Consciousness, Yeshu Abba Consciousness, community consciousness, and to enable us to realise that we are the children of God, one with Christ, in his Sonship, and that God is our Father and that we are brothers and sisters belonging to one family.

For the Eucharistic celebration also we follow the same pattern as we did for meditation, breathing in and breathing out in and through Yeshu and Abba, the receiving and giving movement, the process of death and life.

The whole celebration of Eucharist could be classified as offering, consecration, breaking of the bread and sharing. Reading the scripture, homily, singing and all the prayers are expressions of this great Paschal Mystery, the mystery of death and life, the mystery of receiving and giving, the mystery of love, mystery of the eternal life movement between God and Man, between the Father and the Son in the Spirit.

Let all the people sit round in a circle so that every one in the circle will be able to see the others. This circle, this assembly is the church. "Where two or three are gathered together in my name I will be in the midst." In the center of the circle is the altar where Christ is present. This circle represents the cosmos and the altar is the center of the cosmos. Let all those who are in the circle become aware of this.

It is the Spirit of our Lord and Master Jesus Christ who brought us all together as one body. We are going to celebrate a great mystery under signs and symbols. It is a great sacrament. Everything which we do during this celebration must have a sign value, as the way we sit, the things we use, the words we utter, the prayers we recite, the hymns we sing, the symbols we use, the various movements and gestures of the body and the mind, etc. It should be an expression of what we were and what we are and what we will be.

OFFERTORY

The bread and wine is offered on the altar as a sign of our total self-offering. Each individual offers himself in the center of the assembly.

Let us all look at the center of the community, the altar, and with full concentration breathe in and breathe out. While breathing out each one will give himself to the altar and while breathing in receives the other from the altar. Jesus is in the center of the community and I receive the whole community in and through Yeshu and I give myself to the community in and through Abba. While breathing out I give myself as I am with all my good and bad qualities and in the same way while I breathe in, I receive the other, the whole community as they are. In the process of this movement each individual has to undergo the experience of death, total self giving, total surrender, total emptiness, total detachment in order to give birth to community consciousness. When all the members of the community undergo the experience of death and life, then the whole community will experience itself as one body. This is the meaning of the offertory. The one bread on the altar is the symbol of the whole community as one body as the body of Christ. The Spirit of Jesus draws everyone to the altar and forms one body. While breathing in allow the Spirit of Jesus to enter within you and while breathing out allow yourself to be moved by the movement of the Spirit to the altar to Jesus. After a few minutes of silent movement of self-giving and receiving, we can have an offertory song which should express the meaning of the offertory. Now we must experience that we are all together as one body on the altar in the form of bread and wine. We are no more in the circle or around the altar as we were, but we are on the altar as an offering to God the Father. Experience really what it means being together as one body on the altar. Enter into the experience physically, mentally, psychologically and spiritually. Allow the self to enter into this new level of consciousness, new mode of existence. The spirit of our Master, Jesus, will transform us, give us this experience.

CONSECRATION

The Priest offers the bread and wine to God the Father to be consecrated as the body and blood of Jesus Christ. When the bread and wine is elevated from the altar we must really experience that our own body is being elevated from the altar to God the Father. Jesus Christ assumes human nature as his body and this body in which we are members is elevated from the altar which is this world from earth to heaven to the Kingdom of God the Father. As the body of Christ we are elevated from our lower state of consciousness to higher states of consciousness, from the sleeping state, death state, ignorant state, earth-centered state, self-centered state to the wakeful state, immortal state, enlightenment state, heavenly state, or God-centered state.

Through this elevation of our whole being, we are experiencing again the death and life process, total self-giving and receiving, breathing in and breathing out. Continue the meditation with full consciousness, breathing in Yeshu and breathing out Abba. Stay for a while in deep silence experiencing this great movement between God and man and undergo the purification and experience of transformation.

BREAKING OF THE BREAD AND SHARING

The priest breaks this one bread in order that it may be shared with the whole community. The breaking of the bread is the symbol of our body which has been broken into pieces. Each one undergoes the breaking of his own body. I break my body into several pieces and distribute to each one in the community. We eat each other and our own body. We form as one body the body of Christ and we break this body and eat it. Breaking the body is the experience of life. We break ourselves in order to give ourselves to others. When we celebrate the Eucharist if we don't experience this one body consciousness by total self-giving and receiving, then the celebration has no meaning. It will be an empty ritual. What would St. Paul say in this context of the celebration of the Eucharist? You come together here to share the fellowship, to experience that you are the body of Christ and individually members of it. Because there is one bread, we who are many are one body, for we all partake of the one bread.

CONCLUSION

In the offertory, consecration and breaking-sharing we experience the total self-giving and receiving of one another in and through Yeshu and Abba and experience the death and life. Through this celebration of the Paschal Mystery, death and life, we grow in Yeshu Abba Consciousness, we grow in community consciousness, we grow in Cosmic Consciousness. The Eucharistic celebration is an experience of our realization that God is our Father and we are his children, brothers and sisters, one with Christ in his Sonship. From this deep experience of Yeshu Abba Consciousness, the spirit of

Yeshu-Abba will pray within our spirit, the prayer which Jesus our Lord and Master taught us. "Our Father who art in heaven, Hallowed be thy name. Thy kingdom come, Thy will be done, on earth as it is in heaven. Give us this day our daily bread. And forgive us our debts, as we also have forgiven our debtors. And lead us not into temptation, but deliver us from evil." (Mt. 6:8-13).

This experience which we have in meditation as well as in Eucharistic celebration will flow into our daily activities. After the meditation and Eucharistic celebration we start our work according to each one's charism and profession. Some will go to work in the field, some in factories, some in a school, some in a hospital, some to administration in an office. Here also as a Yogi one has to follow the same pattern as in meditation and Eucharistic celebration. One must give oneself totally in service of others; one must die for others, one must shed his blood for others. That means total self-giving and receiving in and through Yeshu and Abba; accepting one another's love and care for one another. Death and life, breaking of oneself and sharing must be experienced in every activity of life, in meditation, in Eucharistic celebration, in common prayer and in work.

These three ways of Yoga are named Jnana Yoga, Bhakti Yoga and Karma Yoga. Jnana Yoga is study and meditations. Bhakti Yoga is devotion, Eucharistic celebration, etc. Karma Yoga is work. One has to acquire gradually the harmony of these three Yogas and then one will be the perfect human being.

PART X

MARRIAGE BETWEEN RELIGIONS

PART X

MARRIAGE BETWEEN RELIGIONS

It is our experience in India today, that people who belong to various religions live together, eat together, study together and work together but pray separately. For prayer one will go to the Temple, another will go to the Church and another will go to the Mosque. In practice, religion or God becomes the dividing force between religion and religion, nation and nation. It should have been the contrary. Religion or God must be the uniting force, bringing people together in harmony. As we know today so much fighting is going on all over the world, mostly in the name of religion and God. Today, many young people would say that the present type of religion and concept of God must die in order to give birth to a true religion and God.

In 1973 during my pilgrimage from Kanyakumari to the Himalayas I stayed for a week in Bombay and gave a short course on Yoga meditation to some sisters. One afternoon in Bandra I was passing through a small junction and I heard someone calling me, 'Swamiji, Swamiji'. Without noticing I walked still further but the voice continued. So I turned back and saw the house and the man who was calling me. I asked him what he wanted. He invited me to his house. So I went. Some people were there. We all sat together and started to converse. The man told me since many months he was suffering from stomach pain and he had some check-up and treatment but the pain remained. He said that I could do something for him. From this I realized that he had a strong faith in God and God wanted to use me as an instrument for his cure. He opened himself to me. From their names I found out that the others were all Hindus. They were young people, taxi drivers, and they were so sincere that they explained to me what immoral life they lead and the circumstances which forced them to do so.

I told the sick man to lie down on the ground and then I spoke to him the following words. "Now you are going to take a new birth from Bhoomi Devi, the Mother Earth. Earth is your mother. You are going to become one with the earth. The Bhoomi Devi has the power to purify you. Allow yourself to be burnt in the fire of God. Through Bhoomi Devi you can reach God and she will heal you and she will give you a new life. She is our life-giving mother. So you remain here watching your slow movement of breath which God breathes out to you. God sends his power through his breath and purifies you." He remained in that state for fifteen minutes. After that he became more and more aware of his body and slowly he got up and said that he had no stomach pain and he felt some interior joy and peace.

Then we all sat round and continued our prayer. They brought some sweet bread and a bottle of Coca Cola. We kept that in the center and prayed for half an hour singing the

Name of God and had some silent meditation. While we were calling on the Name of God, we felt that the Lord was coming to us and taking us all together as one body and sharing his inner life of love, joy . . . and peace with us. After the singing and meditating, while we were in silence I took the bread and offered it to God, praying Oh! God! Accept this offering which is an expression of our love and concern for one another. And then I broke the bread and we all ate it. I explained the meaning of it; that the one bread represented our unity and belonging to one another, by breaking and eating we share one another in the presence of God.

I took the bottle of Coca Cola and offered it to God and we all drank from it. They expressed their gratitude saying, although they were eleven years in Bombay this was the first time they prayed and experienced God. They asked me to come the following day also. They said: "When Swamiji is with us there is no difficulty to pray, but when Swamiji goes away we are afraid whether we may go back into our old habits." I encouraged them and said, "Have faith in God and he will send his Spirit and the Spirit will help you to pray. Repeat every day at least in the evening before you go to bed and in the morning when you get up the name of God." We thanked God for all the gifts he had bestowed on us and wished good-bye to each other.

The experiences and expressions of two religions are varied and sometimes contradict each other, though there is one God and both religions experience the same God. Even the experience of two persons who belong to the same religion would differ.

Let us go into the expressions of the experiences of some of the major religions. We have to remember that experience of

God cannot be expressed adequately in language. Shankara, one of the important Hindu philosophers, expresses his experiences of God as advaitam 'not two'. For him God and man are 'not two'. God and the world are 'not two.' It takes us days and months of meditation to understand what he means by 'not two'. It is a beautiful and wise way of expressing the experience of God. There is always a tendency for us to come to a conclusion and judgement about it too soon.

A Hindu expresses his experience as 'Aham Brahmasmi', 'I am Brahman'. He experiences Brahman (God) as everything. When he compares himself in relation to Brahman he is nothing, he feels himself to be nothing because Brahman is so great, so he says, 'I am Brahman'. It does not mean that he is not there, but the emphasis is given to Brahman. The mere fact that he said 'I am Brahman', shows that 'I' is there. That means 'I' consciously experience Brahman. 'I' has not lost its identity but it is there in Brahman.

A Hindu seeker who is in search of reality asks this question: Is the earth real? The answer, 'Neti Neti', not this, not this. Is the heaven real? Neti Neti. Is man real? Neti Neti. Everything that he could see and perceive with his senses and intellect is not real. Then he transcends the world of senses, time, matter and space and discovers the reality and says, 'Tat Sat' That is true. That which is beyond is the reality. Then he comes back to the world of senses and says 'Sarvam Idham Brahmam', everything is Brahman, everything is real, earth is real, water is real, air is real, fire is real, heaven is real, animal is real, man is real, everything which he sees and perceives is real. If we take the great sayings, Neti Neti, Tat sat and Sarvam Idham Brahmam together we will get the reality. This is his expression of the experience of God.

Buddha couldn't find any ordinary religious terminology, such as God, reality, ultimate truth to express adequately his experience of God. So he says, 'Sunyata' nothingness. It is nothingness for any human language. This is the way he expresses his experience of God.

St. Paul's experience of God is that "It is not I who live but Christ lives in me." It doesn't mean that St. Paul is not living but the emphasis is given to the life of Christ. He finds his life in Christ through the experience of death. He has to die in order to give birth to the life of Christ in him. This saying is very similar to 'Aham Brahmasmi.' I am Brahman.

Christ's experience of God is expressed as "I and the Father are one, the Father is in me and I in the Father." That is Christ's experience of God as his Father and himself as his beloved son. His relation to God is as son to the Father. "I and the Father are one." "The Father is in me and I in the Father." The Father remains always as Father and the Son remains as Son. The Son never takes the place of the Father but they are one. "He who sees me sees the Father." He is the self-manifestation of the Father. Jesus sees the whole of humanity in relation with him to the Father when he says, "Father, that they all may be one in us as you are in me and I in You." The whole of humanity as the children of God becoming one with his Sonship enters into this Father-Son relationship with God.

There is a common question which normally a Christian would ask. If all religions are worshipping the same God and if all will have salvation, then what is the need for conversion? Then what is the meaning of Jesus' teaching, "Go and preach the good news to the whole world, and baptise those who believe, in the name of the Father, Son and Holy Spirit"? Christians of former times thought that Christianity was the only true religion and the Christian God is the one true God and all other religions are evil and their God is not the true God. The Christian missionary attempted to present the Hindu religion and religious practices in India as something evil in order to establish the Christian religion as interpreted by the Graeco-Roman mind. They misinterpreted the great sayings such as 'Advaita', 'Aham Brahmasmi', 'Neti Neti', 'Tat Sat', 'Sarvam Idam Brahmam', 'Sunyata' as saying in Hinduism everything is God, man is claiming himself to be God, or the world is not real for them. Or in Buddhism there is no God. The Hindu, they thought, worships nature, the sun, the moon, the stars, the fire, water, trees, mountains, animals, etc.

After the Second Vatican Council there is a great change in the understanding of the Catholic Church in its attitude towards other religions. Now we believe that anyone who believes in God and practices his religion will have salvation. There is only one God and all religions are moving towards Him.

What should be our attitude towards other religions? Do we still continue to preach the good news, the way and how I find fulfilment in this way? For example, first of all I am an Indian Christian. Hindu religion is my own religion. As an Indian it is my birthright to possess this religion and practise this religion. God was revealing himself in India from the beginning of the creation. The great teachings of the Rishis and Sages of this country are the outcome of their experience of God's intervention in their lives. The Hindu religion is the religion of the people who are in the process of the experience of God and enlightenment.

Man is a social being and men live for one another. Human love means giving oneself fully to the other and receiving the other. Take the example of a Hindu and a Christian. The Hindu is having the experience of God as Saccidananda; truth, consciousness and bliss. The Christian is having the experience of God as Father, Son and Holy Spirit. As a Hindu I give myself to you as I am. That means I cannot separate my experience of God as Saccidananda from me. My whole being is in that experience. In the same way with open heart I receive you as a Christian as you are with all your experience of God as Father-Son-Holy Spirit which is in your whole being. Now the Hindu experience of God and the Christian experience of God meets within me. The marriage is the best symbol through which we can explain this meeting. The marriage of Hindu and Christian experiences takes place in me. A man and woman enter into marriage. But after the marriage man never becomes woman and woman never becomes man. Man never loses his identity as man and woman never loses her identity as woman. Both were married together as one body and share everything together and grow together without losing their own identity that is unity in diversity.

In the same way, as a Hindu, when I experience God as Father-Son-Holy Spirit, I will not lose my experience of God as Saccidananda. My experience of Saccidananda will not be a hindrance for me to experience God as Father-Son and Holy Spirit; rather the two experiences enrich each other. Christians have always a fear, if they are open to other religions, that they will lose their identity, their faith, their experience. It is only a fear. When a Hindu and a Christian meet together with mutual understanding and openness and total self-giving in love, the fear will disappear and the marriage of the two distinct religious experiences take place.

It is not syncretism or mixing two different religious

experiences but it is a marriage. Each religion is unique. One religion is not the same as the other religion. There is a tendency in Hinduism to say that all religions are the same and Shiva, Krishna, Allah, Buddha and Christ all are the same. But we must be very clear in our mind that each religion is unique, not the same. It is very important for interreligious dialogue.

Each religion has its universal aspect and the duty to share its unique experience of God with all people just out of love and concern for one another. In that sense Christianity has its unique experience of God and this experience has to be preached to all mankind. The greatest teaching of Jesus is love for God and for one another.

With regard to the revelation of God there is no superiority or inferiority. Christians often think that their religion is superior to all other religions. From the beginning of the creation God was continuously revealing himself to all men under various symbols and signs. As men we have no right to make any judgement on it. Each religion and each experience is unique. And each revelation is conditioned by time, place, culture and the mind of the people. Let us have the humility to accept the way it is revealed. Each religion has its unique function. The only thing that I have to do is that, what I experienced, what I am convinced of and what I believe, I put into practice and share with my fellow men. And I must be totally open to other men to receive what they offer to me. God reveals himself to me through the spirit who is within me and through the spirit who is within other men. I must be totally ready to welcome God in the way which he comes to me.